Teaching Multilingual Learners in Rural Schools

Four Movements for Educators

Maria R. Coady
with contributions by
Cassandra Rubinstein

Routledge
Taylor & Francis Group
NEW YORK AND LONDON

Designed cover image: Getty Images

First published 2027
by Routledge
605 Third Avenue, New York, NY 10158

and by Routledge
4 Park Square, Milton Park, Abingdon, Oxon, OX14 4RN

Routledge is an imprint of the Taylor & Francis Group, an informa business

ISBN: 978-1-032-79806-6 (pbk)
ISBN: 978-1-003-50987-5 (ebk)

DOI: 10.4324/9781003509875

Typeset in Palatino
by SPi Technologies India Pvt Ltd (Straive)

Teaching Multilingual Learners in Rural Schools

Teaching Multilingual Learners in Rural Schools is a call to action and a guide to empower educators to build strong, just, and multilingual rural communities.

The book offers a research-informed framework for transforming how rural schools serve multilingual learners (MLs). Using the metaphor of a symphony, the author organizes the work around four "movements": Representation and Belonging, Shared Vision, Centering Families, and Collaboration. Each movement harmonizes research, policy, and practice to create equity-driven learning environments where rural ML students can thrive academically and socially.

Set against today's rapidly changing educational landscape, this resource provides educators and policymakers with strategies for designing inclusive, locally grounded programs. Through case studies, field insights, and reflective questions, you will discover how rural schools can honor place, language, and identity while advancing excellence and opportunity for all learners.

Maria R. Coady, Ph.D., is the Goodnight Distinguished Professor in Education and Professor of Multilingual Education at North Carolina State University. With over three decades of experience in multilingual education, Dr. Coady is a leading voice in rural education equity and advocacy for English learners.

Equity and Social Justice in Education Series

Paul C. Gorski, Series Editor

Routledge's Equity and Social Justice in Education series is a publishing home for books that apply critical and transformative equity and social justice theories to the work of on-the-ground educators. Books in the series describe meaningful solutions to the racism, white supremacy, economic injustice, sexism, heterosexism, transphobia, ableism, neoliberalism, and other oppressive conditions that pervade schools and school districts.

Transformative Mindfulness in Education
Caring for Ourselves While Kindling Change
Rhiannon Kim

Teaching Indigenous Studies
An Introduction for K-12 Educators
Leilani Sabzalian, Meredith McCoy, and Helen Thomas

Peacebuilding Pedagogies
Racial Justice, Dialogue, and Belonging in the Classroom
Crystena Parker-Shandal

Cultivating Critical Advocacy
A Framework for Educators of Multilingual Learners
Rebecca E. Linares and Kate Seltzer

The DEI Practitioner's Handbook
A Guide for School and District Leaders in Pursuit of Educational Justice
Erica Buchanan-Rivera

Teaching Multilingual Learners in Rural Schools
Four Movements for Educators
Maria R. Coady

Dr. Maria R. Coady

In loving memory of Dr. Rosa Castro-Feinberg (1939–2026), my academic mother and mentor, colleague, ally, and friend, whose generous spirit, profound wisdom, and lifelong dedication to multilingual learners touched countless lives and transformed our field. Her legacy endures in all who continue the work she loved.

Cassandra Rubinstein

To Dr. Coady and the mentors who shine light through systems too often designed to obscure—whose conviction sustains our resolve, whose questions sharpen our thinking, and whose unwavering support taught me that scholarship and care are inseparable. And to all who labor toward schools where every child belongs—the teachers, the leaders, and the communities who insist that education remain a site of possibility. May we continue to build what we have not yet imagined.

Contents

Meet the Author

Maria R. Coady, PhD, is the Goodnight Distinguished Professor in Education and Professor of Multilingual Education at North Carolina State University. With over three decades of experience in multilingual education, Dr. Coady is a leading voice in rural education equity and advocacy for English learners. Her groundbreaking research examines the intersections of multilingual education, rural education, language policy, and teacher preparation in rural and underserved communities across the United States and internationally.

Dr. Coady's scholarship has been recognized with numerous prestigious awards, including the American Educational Research Association *Exemplary Contributions to Practice-Engaged Research Award* (2020) and the *Leadership through Research* Award from the Second Language Research Special Interest Group (2024). She has directed multiple federally funded projects, including Project STELLAR (Supporting Teachers of English Language Learners Across Rural Settings), a $2.4 million initiative aimed at improving educational outcomes for rural multilingual students and Project DELTA, examining the relationship between preservice teacher preparation and EL learning outcomes.

As a Fulbright Distinguished Chair and Specialist Scholar, Dr. Coady has collaborated with educators and researchers in Poland, South Africa, and Ukraine, bringing global perspectives to her work on multilingual education. She is the founding president of both the Florida Association for Bilingual Education (FABE) and the Carolina Association for Bilingual Education (CarABE), and currently serves on the Executive Board of the National Association for Bilingual Education (NABE) as the Eastern Region Representative and as Interim President of ASPIRA of the Mid Atlantic.

Dr. Coady is the author of several influential books, including *The Coral Way Bilingual Program* (2020), *Connecting School and the Multilingual Home: Theory and Practice for Rural Educators* (2019), and *Educating Multilingual Learners in Rural Schools: Illuminating Diversity in Rural Communities in the United States* (with P. Golombek and N. Marichal). Her work has appeared in top-tier journals such as *Educational Researcher*, *TESOL Quarterly*, and the *Bilingual Research Journal*. She has also produced documentary films exploring the experiences of immigrant families and undocumented youth, including *Small Town, Big Dreams* and *Long Journey to the American Dream*.

A passionate advocate for educational equity, Dr. Coady serves as president of the Foundation for Language Education and Development (LEAD), a nonprofit organization providing scholarships to underserved students pursuing higher education. She also serves as an expert consultant to the U.S. Department of Justice and Office for Civil Rights on English learner education matters.

Before joining NC State in 2022, Dr. Coady was the Irving and Rose Fien Endowed Professor at the University of Florida, where she served as ESOL/Bilingual Education Program Coordinator and directed numerous teacher preparation initiatives. She earned her Ph.D. in Social, Bilingual and Multicultural Foundations of Education from the University of Colorado Boulder as a U.S. Department of Education Title VII Fellow, her M.Ed. from Boston University, and her B.S. from the University of New Hampshire.

Dr. Coady lives in Raleigh, North Carolina, where she continues her commitment to transforming educational opportunities for multilingual learners (MLs) in rural communities. Through her scholarship, advocacy, and community engagement, she works to ensure that all students, regardless of their linguistic background or geographic location, have access to equitable, high-quality education.

Preface

The sun—in its lazy winter rise—is barely on the horizon this cold winter morning. When I open the kitchen blind, the frost on the grass glistens like diamonds where the light touches it. In the distance, between the rooftops, I can see the tall church steeple in the village, just past the *boulangerie* and Café des Arts. As the sun warms the earth, birds chatter and search for seeds amidst the otherwise peaceful silence. I smell the earthy, smoky, damp aroma of burning peat, which warms the nearby houses.

This region in western France is dotted with fields of wheat, corn, rye, and the magnificent golden flaxseed that emerges in springtime. Traversing the countryside are industries that produce bread and flour, and poultry. Close to the Atlantic, locals harvest sea salt from the marshes, along with oysters and mussels pulled fresh from the tides. There is a regionalism across France that is integral to and emphasizes each area's culture, food, and history. Locals are proud of the *terroir*—that untranslatable concept encompassing soil, climate, and tradition—that shapes their everyday lives.

People here take their relationship to the land seriously. The village recycling center is meticulously managed and staffed, with each section dedicated to recycling or renewal: papers and boxes, *graviers* (gravels), *déchet vert* (yard waste), electronics, glass, and plastics—rigid or soft—to be separated accordingly. Although I have made several mistakes sorting my recyclables, and am quick to be corrected, the commitment to preserving the land, the regional strengths and products, and history bring me hope.

I have come to France to write, to think, and to find perspective. Distance—geographical and temporal—has a way of clarifying what matters most. Surrounded by a landscape where people have cultivated the same crops for generations, where the rhythm of life is still set by seasons and soil, I find myself returning again and again to a fundamental question: What are we—who are we—if not people inhabiting land and renewing, daily, our relationship to it and to each other? Antonín Dvořák, the famous composer whose work is paralleled throughout this book, also knew this and reflected this principle in his uniquely American *From the New World* symphony.

This question sits at the heart of this book. It is a question that rural communities across the world understand intuitively, even as broader society often overlooks or has forgotten this wisdom. Rural people know that identity is shaped by place, that knowledge is rooted in context, and that community is built through sustained relationships with neighbors, tradition, and the land itself.

***

This book is a dedication to rural educators and the critical work that we do in uplifting diverse people and honoring the inextricable relationship that we have to the land we share. It is written for teachers in small towns and rural and remote communities who see multilingual students not as problems to be solved but as assets to be celebrated. It is written for administrators navigating impossible budget constraints while still fighting for equity and equality. It is written for families whose languages and cultures represent generations of knowledge, and for communities whose strengths have too long been rendered invisible by deficit-oriented narratives.

In the current moment, our task is made more challenging by deep financial cuts to public education—including the elimination of the U.S. Department of Education and the Office of English Language Acquisition—threats to diverse peoples and particularly those from immigrant backgrounds, and the systematic removal of historical references from source materials. The policy landscape has shifted beneath our feet, and many of the federal supports that once existed for MLs have been dismantled or defunded. Rural communities, already stretched thin, now face these challenges with fewer resources and less institutional backing than ever before.

And yet rural educators are resourceful. They have always done more with less, built coalitions where none existed, and found ways to serve students whom others forgot. The current moment demands that we draw upon these strengths—not in spite of our rural contexts, but precisely because of them.

Rural Cultural Wealth for multilingual students is more than a theory or idea: it is a roadmap for navigating education that includes rather than excludes, uplifts rather than oppresses, and builds rather than eliminates. It recognizes that rural communities possess unique forms of capital—aspirational, navigational, social, linguistic, familial, and resistant—that have sustained diverse peoples across generations. It insists that place matters, that local knowledge is valuable, and that the families and communities surrounding our schools are partners in the educational enterprise, not obstacles to it.

The chapters that follow offer both conceptual frameworks and practical guidance. They draw on research, as well as the lived experiences of rural educators, multilingual families, and community members who have generously shared their stories with me over the years. This book does not offer easy answers, because there are none. What it offers instead is a vision—a vision of rural schools as spaces of belonging, of MLs as contributors rather than recipients, and of educators as advocates capable of transforming systems even when those systems resist transformation.

Our task is not easy, but it is nonetheless essential—and perhaps more so now than ever. In a time of division, rural communities remind us that we are bound to one another and to the places we call home. In a time of erasure, multilingual families remind us that language is heritage, identity, and possibility all at once. In times of despair, educators remind us that hope is not passive—it is built daily in classrooms and communities where people support one another.

Like the farmers of western France who tend their fields season after season, like the villagers who meticulously sort their recyclables in service of generations yet to come, we too are engaged in work that requires patience, persistence, and hope in the future. The harvest is not always immediate. The results are not always visible. But our work matters.

I hope that this book serves as both a resource and a reminder: You are not alone, your work matters, and the communities you serve are rich with possibility.

Vendée, France
January 5, 2026

1

Introduction

Four Educational Movements for Rural Multilingual Learner Education

> A country best expresses itself when it reaches deep down into its own musical traditions.
>
> —*Bukowski (Banther & Bukowski, 2021)*

Introduction

Imagine you are a teacher in a remote rural school district. Driving to school in the morning, you pass fields of yellowing corn stalks swaying in the early fall breeze. The sun reaches over the horizon. The sounds of cattle and the smell of pine invigorate your senses. You breathe in the morning dew. The road narrows as you turn into the long, rocky driveway leading to the brick U-shaped school building. The energy of children being dropped off early to school, laughing and running for the playground, is palpable. The school sits alone on the road, set back from commerce and public buildings. But even in its aloneness, the school is clearly a shared community space. You see people gather and work together to benefit the community and the children. Its presence holds the histories and cultures of the people who have inhabited this place for hundreds of years, and who survived on

DOI: 10.4324/9781003509875-1

the land, with the land, and sometimes in spite of the land. Land is integral to rurality. Like the *terroir*—a French term that refers to a 'sense of place' and the characteristics of that place (Howley & Howley, 2014)—this community, too, has a story to tell. It has borne witness to decades of diverse students—from Indigenous backgrounds to newcomer migrant worker families who travel to harvest crops and stay to work on dairy and hog farms. What stories does this school hold? As you look, you wonder: Whose stories are portrayed on the walls or spoken in the halls? What role do I have as a teacher in shaping the school community and the stories it tells?

I recently conducted fieldwork, which included a linguistic landscape analysis, in a rural community called Campton (pseudonym), in a southeastern state of the United States. A linguistic landscape analysis is an examination of how different languages are utilized in the physical environment of a specific community space. Examples of the material environment include cultural artifacts, signage, and other print or written documentation that are frequently passed by without much notice. However, the material environment of a place contributes to the story that it tells about the people who live there.

Using a linguistic landscape observation tool (see Figure 1.1), I documented the imagery, commercial signs, bulletin board invitations, business cards tacked onto boards, fliers, and invitations from the town's public library, coffee shop, Chamber of Commerce, and local businesses. I took extensive photographs and field notes surrounding the use (or absence of) minoritized languages to understand how people from various language backgrounds "show up" and are portrayed in rural communities, if at all.

The rural community I visited bears little resemblance to the one described in the opening paragraph of this chapter. The local crop industry in Campton is tobacco, and the *terroir* is influenced by prolonged, humid periods of weather, abundant sunlight, and a unique soil composition that affects the growth of the tobacco plant. Workers harvest the tobacco and hang it to dry. The fall county fair celebrates the tobacco harvest and hosts local agriculture competitions that include hog and poultry. Like the opening

Linguistic Landscape Observation Tool

[Adapted from Gorter (2006), "linguistic landscape refers to the social context in which more than one language is present. It implies the use in speech or writing of more than one language and thus of multilingualism" (p. 1)].

Community, town, school, or location	
People present (students, families, community members)	
Date	
Language(s) identified	
Time start and end	

For each site or venue, describe and/or sketch the setting: Who was present? What languages were used–spoken or written?

Document the images taken of the linguistic landscape, noting time, place, languages, people, and description of the image. 1. 2. 3. 4. 5. 6.

FIGURE 1.1 Linguistic landscape observation tool. Adapted from Gorter (2006), "linguistic landscape refers to the social context in which more than one language is present. It implies the use in speech or writing of more than one language and thus of multilingualism" (p. 1).

vignette of this chapter, the community of Campton in the southeast U.S. is considered rural and has a rural school grounded in history, the land, and the people who inhabit the region.

The school is situated approximately a half mile (one kilometer) from a small downtown area. The downtown has two intersecting main streets—a primary pass-through where large trucks and cars barrel through each day without stopping. The cross street is home to a coffee shop, a thrift store, a local chamber of commerce building, and a one-room public library divided into sections featuring books of various genres and a young children's area. At the library entrance is an information board depicting local community events, the dates of the annual fall tobacco harvest festival, and the family story times available during the week for English-speaking families. Outside the library, at the far end of the cross street, there is a single Mexican restaurant, the only visible representation of a language other than English in the town. Both Campton and the community described in the opening vignette are designated rural in the federal locale classification system and have rural schools. However, they are distinctly different in terms of the *terroir*, how the communities function, the stories revealed about the people, and the relationship between the people and land.

While the term *rural* frequently conjures images of bucolic farmscapes, lush harvests, and farmers with pitchforks reminiscent of Wood's *American Gothic* painting, rural areas are each unique. In the United States, rural communities are also increasingly culturally, racially, linguistically, and industrially diverse (Bennett et al., 2019; Lichter & Johnson, 2020). Diverse people are present in all areas of the country. For the first time in the history of the U.S., the national population under the age of 10 is majority non-White, and people of color currently make up more than 20% of the rural population (Lichter et al., 2018; Pipa & Geismar, 2020). More specifically, demographers Lichter and Johnson (2020) have attributed the trend of rural repopulation to immigrant Latinos, referring to this group as a "demographic lifeline" (p. 785) for rural community functioning. The children of rural Latino immigrants attend local public schools, participate in community cultural and sporting events, and contribute to the economic well-being of their towns (Azano et al., 2025). Yet we should ask: how are their languages and cultures portrayed in rural schools? This chapter focuses on that key question, which frames the ideas, theories, and practices described throughout this book.

The quote at the beginning of this chapter captures the relationship between a people (country) and its traditions (or culture) and captures the essence of work with rural multilingual learner (ML) students. Education for *rural* MLs has been largely overlooked in the educational literature for decades. Rurality has not been addressed in a meaningful, systematic way for ML students (Coady, 2020), either in research or in teacher or leader preparation programs. In fact, the term "rurality" has become almost synonymous with 'placelessness' in educational research. Too many scholars who have worked in rural communities describe the context of their studies with a curt sentence: 'this study took place in a rural community'. The lack of context, rich and grounded description, and connection to place has tragic implications for education because it fails to acknowledge the strengths and knowledge rooted in place. One reason for this, perhaps, is that research and educator preparation in rural education have not intersected with research and practices in ML education. These two areas remain disparate and siloed. So, while we have a growing body of research on 'rural education' and significant knowledge surrounding 'ML (or English learner) education', the intersection of these two areas is sparse at best (Coady, 2020).

At the time of writing this book, in late 2025, the landscape for both rural and ML education has been shifting in significant ways, with these changes playing out in real-time decisions for rural MLs and families. Federal policies, such as Executive Order 14224 signed by President Donald Trump on March 1, 2025, declaring English as the official national language, have rippling effects on how schools interpret and provide language-learning services for non-native English speakers in U.S. schools. Threats to high-quality programs, like dual language immersion (DLI) for ML students, and supplemental resources that were intended to address vast funding disparities between rural and nonrural schools, are facing unprecedented challenges.

In 2025, the federal government proposed closing the U.S. Department of Education entirely and eliminating the Rural Education Achievement Program (REAP)—about $220 million of funding that went to rural schools through two programs, the Small Rural School Achievement Program and the Rural and Low-Income School (RLIS) program. In addition to those rural-designated programs, the U.S. Office of English Language Acquisition (OELA), which oversaw educational programs and services for 5.3 million identified ML students, was shuttered. For rural schools that used this targeted funding, these are significant financial losses (Coady, 2025).

Unless individual U.S. states redesignate the federal block funding that they receive from the federal government for those programs by providing parallel funding and earmarking those funds for rural schools and ML students, rural MLs will struggle significantly and are not likely to receive the language-learning supports required to learn and thrive. This is the context in which rural education for ML students operates today. This means that now more than ever, rural educators must come together in shared vision, unity, strength, and commitment to serve the country's most vulnerable students. This book aims to forge a path forward through the educational policy chaos to ensure that rural ML students are not overlooked or forgotten.

Demographics and Indicators

Currently, across the U.S., there are more than nine million kindergarten through grade 12 students who attend rural schools (NCES, 2023a). There are about 5.3 million identified ML students in total (NCES, 2023b). Data from the National Center for Educational Statistics (NCES, 2023c) indicate that, according to the locale classification system (rural, small town, suburban, and urban spaces), there are approximately 350,000 MLs at the intersection of rural and ML students (Table 1.1). However, these numbers don't always capture rural school districts with low numbers of ML students, who are not required to be reported, nor do they account for how ML students are identified and exited from supplemental language-learning services. These practices vary across the 50 U.S. states, making it more challenging to determine the precise number of rural MLs.

TABLE 1.1 Growth in rural ML students 2003–2022

School year	*Rural ML students*	*MLs as % of rural enrollment*
2003–04	~230,000	2.4
2015–16	~272,000	3.6
2019–20	~327,000	4.4
2021–22	~356,000	4.8

Sources: NCES *Status of Education in Rural America* (2007) for 2003–2004; NCES Digest Table 214.40 (2015–2019); NCES Condition of Education "English Learners in Public Schools" (2021–2022).

There remain further differences across U.S. states in the identification processes for language-learning services for ML students, as required under current federal law. In my home state of North Carolina, the 2024 "headcount"—literally the counting of students present in the classroom who qualify for ML services—was about 178,000. This number increased from 164,000 in 2023, marking a 9.2% increase in one year (NC DPI, 2024). In 2025, for the first time in decades, the number of MLs *dropped* to about 163,175. This decrease was likely the result of the state lowering the cut score on the standardized test (the WIDA ACCESS test) and the loss of immigrant-background ML students due to the federal government's immigration enforcement escalation (Najarro & Harwin, 2025).

The landscape of American education—and, specifically, rural ML education—is changing rapidly and without precedent. The current anti-immigrant context is affecting local, state, and federal policies and politics. Families and their children face the fear and trauma of an uncertain future. Schools, like hospitals and churches, are no longer considered safe spaces for children and families (Pearson, 2024). Families from immigrant backgrounds who are here fear for their livelihoods and family unity. At the same time, from outside of the U.S., new immigrants are not arriving in the numbers experienced before 2025. According to a recent article, the number of immigrants crossing the southern U.S. border has fallen significantly (Aleaziz, 2025).

In addition to these contextual challenges, ML students may be inaccurately placed in special education programs rather than receiving targeted English language-learning services.

These challenges occur in rural and nonrural communities alike. However, rural communities with limited resources, costly transportation, and fewer prepared educators for linguistic diversity face added challenges in adequately serving rural MLs (Coady, 2020; Coady & Román, 2024).

For instance, the number of language-prepared educators for rural MLs is exceptionally low, and programs to meet their needs are spotty. Data from the National Teacher and Principal Survey (U.S. ED, 2016) indicate that only 62.7% of rural MLs participated in instruction designed to address their language-learning needs, despite more than four decades of federal guidelines requiring research-based language-learning programs for MLs. Under the Fifth Circuit Court of Appeals, *Castañeda v. Pickard* (1981) (648 F.2d) case, school districts must provide a research-informed language education program and evaluate the effectiveness of the program.

As of a decade ago, only 5% of rural U.S. high schools offered bilingual instruction for ML students, and only 50% provided English as a second language (ESL) instruction as a scheduled class for MLs (Lewis & Gray, 2016). These data indicate that rural ML students have less access to high-quality language-learning programs, services, and prepared teachers, which research has repeatedly shown to support their English language development. The domino effect of this means that rural educators, who play complex and multifaceted roles in rural schools (Moffa & McHenry-Sorber, 2018), are often underprepared to provide the instruction, services, and family engagement practices that facilitate language and content learning, improve dropout rates among rural MLs, and support rural ML students' social and emotional well-being.

The Consistently Positive Outcomes of Bilingual Education

The past 25 years have witnessed a significant expansion of research on MLs as a field. This includes educational programs and practices that demonstrate effective outcomes, as documented repeatedly by scholars and supported by the National

Clearinghouse for English Language Acquisition (NCELA). NCELA, operating under OELA, has collected decades of research showing positive practices that improve learning outcomes for MLs, including those participating in bilingual education programs. However, to underscore, there has been very little scholarship on the role of place and the unique challenges and strengths of rural schools, or on the effective practices that support the learning of rural ML students. Disparities in funding for rural schools, lower rural family income levels, and issues of language, race, and ethnicity contribute to disparities in access to high-quality educational programs and services.

In my work in rural schools, which are funded under a public-school model in which local property taxes provide the base, some districts have resorted to using technology tools such as Rosetta Stone and Duolingo to replace ESL teachers. While these programs may provide some language-learning support for travelers to engage in everyday conversation in another country, they are insufficient to provide the academic language-learning support necessary for MLs to participate in content-area classrooms. Education for MLs requires building rigorous and precise academic vocabulary, oracy, and literacy skills in order to learn academic content. Those skills are best developed in collaboration with first language oracy and literacy (Escamilla et al., 2014, 2022), such as in a bilingual education program, which builds ML students' linguistic repertoire and transfers to English language development.

Too often, rural ESL teachers whose task is to develop language skills end up conducting "homework triage" for ML students. That is, they spend significant time assisting students in completing their work in content-area classes, with little time remaining for English language development. In contrast to homework triage, in an ESL model of instruction, ML students should have access to an ESL curriculum that systematically develops language and literacy. For rural schools, the need for additional ESL and language-prepared teachers is pressing. Rural schools with limited resources for ESL teachers and services often require ESL teachers to travel long distances between schools. Rural ESL teachers lament that there are not enough of them, and that they spend their time with the ML students who have the highest learning needs, generally those at the beginning levels of English language learning.

While more common in rural communities than bilingual education programs, ESL programs show among the least positive outcomes for ML students overall (Thomas & Collier, 2002). One thing we know, however, is that there have been consistently positive outcomes for ML students when their first language is used as a medium of instruction for learning English (Coady & Sorel, 2019; McField & McField, 2014). While it may seem counterintuitive that more use of a student's non-English first language would lead to better outcomes, research consistently demonstrates this to be true. A large and growing body of empirical studies demonstrates that a student's use of their home language(s) in school is associated with positive educational outcomes (Collier & Thomas, 2017). One way that this occurs is by assessing what students know, speak, use, and are literate in, and using their language as a resource for understanding and continued learning.

Scholars such as García (2024) and Escamilla et al. (2014) show how opening **linguistic spaces** in classrooms and schools has a positive effect on ML students' identity development and learning. Additional benefits show that student learning improves with the use of the home language for learning academic content, as in DLI programs, and increases MLs' sense of belonging and home-school relationships. Home language use in school affirms MLs' identities, builds positive relationships with diverse families with rich cultural and linguistic backgrounds, and leads to improved learning when MLs' overall linguistic repertoire is activated. We will discuss these ideas further and provide numerous examples of "what this looks like" in the following four chapters of this book.

Monolingual frameworks that are used to identify services and provide support for MLs are very often inadequate because they are not designed for multilingual learners (August & Shanahan, 2006; Carrillo Carrasquillo et al., 2026). Finally, we know that home socioeconomic status has a strong correlation to student learning outcomes, and this holds for ML students.

Students from low-wealth backgrounds face disproportionate challenges that affect language development, learning, and well-being. Because rural communities are home to more low-wealth families (Population Reference Bureau, 2003), there is a greater need for additional funding and support for rural ML students. Rural schools and students can benefit from both equal funding and equitable approaches to education for diverse learners.

Equality and Equity in Rural ML Education

In 2025, federal executive orders mandated the removal of key concepts, including equity, diversity, and inclusion, which impact educational programs for rural minority students (EO 14151). The mandate to remove these concepts and words appears to be based on several misconceptions: first, that rather than forming a unifying and collective American identity, these concepts, individually or together, create division; second, that these concepts have developed something called "the deep state"; and third, that these concepts aim to cause harm or a sense of discomfort among majority groups in the U.S. Counter to these claims, consider these as cornerstones of America: the uplifting of people from varied and diverse backgrounds with respect for each other as human beings and Americans, the understanding that who we are as Americans is rooted in deep histories that are not equally shared by each group or by any individual, and, finally, that inclusion provides everyone an opportunity to participate and a chance to succeed.

When we imagine what schools and classrooms would look like when rural MLs thrive in our schools, we must consider both equality and equity. Equality focuses on providing rural students with the same resources and opportunities as their urban and suburban peers. At the same time, equity ensures those resources and opportunities are tailored to the unique languages, cultures, and experiences that ML students bring with them.

Equality in rural ML education would begin with fair and consistent funding. Rural schools would receive per-student funding on par with suburban and wealthier districts, making it possible to offer robust programs without being hindered by limited budgets. Staffing would also be equal, with the same ratio of ESL teachers to students found in well-resourced schools. Every rural ML would have access to high-quality ESL teachers and/or bilingual education programs and curriculum designed to support English development while sustaining academic success. Technology gaps, such as limited Internet access or outdated hardware, would no longer exist, closing the digital divide between rural and nonrural schools.

Transportation—often one of the most significant challenges that rural schools face—would be supported through shared state funds, relieving districts of the rising costs of bus maintenance, driver wages, gasoline, and climate adaptation measures such as air conditioning. Transportation would also be flexible, enabling ML students to participate in before- and after-school programs in the same way that suburban and urban students are able to. In addition, all rural educators—not just ESL specialists—would receive regular, high-quality professional development to strengthen their capacity for supporting MLs in every classroom.

Yet equality alone is not enough. Equity in rural ML education means recognizing that students arrive with diverse languages, proficiency levels, and cultural wealth that must shape the design of programs. Equitable instruction ensures that ML students' languages are used as resources for learning and literacy rather than being ignored or viewed as obstacles. It also requires moving beyond monolingual frameworks, such as rigid "science of reading" models, which fail to reflect how multilinguals actually develop language and literacy across multiple languages and literacies. In an equitable system, educators intentionally draw on the cultural and linguistic strengths and knowledge of ML students to guide both teaching practices and advocacy. The voices, backgrounds, and lived experiences of rural MLs would be central to how schools define success.

Together, equality and equity paint a fuller vision for rural ML education. Equality ensures that rural schools are no longer left behind in resources and opportunities. Equity ensures that those resources are responsive to the unique identities of ML students and families. For educators, the task is not just to level the playing field but also to design learning spaces where the languages and cultures of rural ML students are celebrated and are integral to their success. Without doubt, high-quality education for rural ML students must be both equal in terms of educational inputs, such as rural funding, access to resources such as prepared teachers, technology, and equitable—meaning language-specific instruction and support that meet the requirements of legal guidelines such as under the U.S. Supreme Court decision in *Castañeda v. Pickard*, 1981; Coady et al., 2022), which enable MLs to access curriculum and academic content. For rural MLs, this is not an either-or but rather an and/plus proposition.

Four Educational Movements

As an educational scholar, I am committed to meeting educational challenges with research-informed practices that lead to learning and well-being for all students, particularly rural MLs. Over the past 25 years that I have worked with rural ML students, families, and educators, I have collected data and exemplars of the outstanding work of educators who uplift rural community strengths for the betterment of all members of their community and the improvement of learning and well-being for MLs. As I looked back over this work, taking a 10,000-foot bird's-eye view of the portrait that they painted, I noticed four distinct yet interrelated activities that lead to positive outcomes. I refer to these metaphorically as *movements*.

To be clear, I am not a musician beyond my grade four to seven music lessons, where I learned to play the flute in band; however, I can appreciate different interpretations of music. For instance, the renowned jazz musicia, Melody Gardot, performs regularly in four langauges, including a passionate rendition of the song *Moon River*, originally made famous by Audrey Hepburn in the film *Breakfast at Tiffany's* (1961). The song was composed by Henry Mancini and produced by Joe Reisman. In a recent performance, Gardot recounted how Reisman insisted that she record *Moon River*, to which she replied that it had already been sung and beautifully interpreted.

Reisman persisted, and Gardot recorded the song, paying tribute to Reisman, who produced both the first and final versions of the song before his passing. Like musical interpretation, we must understand and interpret our rural context, its unique features and strengths, affordances, and challenges.

Consider the four educational movements in this book like the varied musical compositions that comprise a symphony. A symphony is a multi-movement work of music performed by an orchestra (Layton, 1995). As a singular musical piece, a symphony is typically comprised of four "movements." Each movement serves as a distinct story or "chapter," conveying a specific feeling or sentiment, and contributes to the larger story. In the symphony, the first movement typically serves as an introduction and is an exposition of the theme that may be heard throughout the subsequent movements. It is often lively (*allegro*) music. The second movement is a slower, more lyrical piece, and the composition is reflective, introspective, and invokes a sense of beauty. The third movement is a quick, energetic dance known as a scherzo. The final movement serves as the fast, exciting finale that concludes the work.

The symphonic sonata is akin to a grand narrative, with each movement serving as a distinct chapter in a book that contributes to the overall message. What I enjoy about the symphony is the range of emotions that each movement evokes, as well as the multitude of interpretations of the movements themselves. As each piece is played, it comes alive through the musicians' expertise, knowledge, and interpretation. Similarly, consider these four principles in this book on rural ML education as you interpret them through the strengths, histories, and relationships that frame your rural community.

Symphonies are often misperceived as purely Eurocentric. However, this is not how the first uniquely American symphony came to be. *From the New World* was a masterpiece composed by Czech composer Antonín Dvořák, who came to New York City in 1892 to compose the symphony at the request of philanthropist Jeanette Thurber, who directed the National Conservatory (Smaczny, 1995). Thurber aimed "to incubate the creation and nurture the development of a musical identity for America that would overcome the dominance of European cultural influences" (de Farber, 2021, p. 2).

Dvořák's work was influenced by his humble beginnings and early life experiences. He found inspiration for this work among the diverse people of America, whom he came to know upon his arrival in New York. Dvořák met Harry T. Burleigh, a student at the National Conservatory and the grandson of a former slave who grew up surrounded by Black spiritual music. Dvořák hired Burleigh to assist him in music transcription, and the two became friends. The symbiotic relationship between the two enabled Dvořák to access a range of diverse American music, notably Black spirituals, which he used to create one of his most famous compositions (Banther & Keely, 2024).

Black spirituals, Czech folk melodies, and Native American rhythm are evident throughout the four movements of the New World Symphony (Banther & Bukowski, 2021). In addition to Black spirituals, the symphony is also tied to Native American culture through H. W. Longfellow's epic poem, *Song of Hiawatha*. Aspects of this poem are reminiscent of both the second and third movements of the New World Symphony. The symphony is remarkable because it captures the influences of America's diverse people. A 1893 *New York Herald* news article quotes Dvořák as saying,

> I am convinced that the future music of this country must be founded on what are called Negro melodies. These can be the foundation of a serious and original school of composition to be developed in the United States. These beautiful and varied themes are the product of the soil. They are the folksongs of America, and your composers must turn to them.
>
> *(5′33″–5′54″)*

The New World Symphony has become a testament to American culture, its history, and its people's right to self-expression.

The four movements presented in this practitioner book are designed to demonstrate how principles for rural ML education can be interpreted and applied to meet your needs and those of ML students in your rural community. Dvořák's work as a composer in the 19th-century U.S. is a reminder that who we are today is a result of those who came before us. Your task is to locate cultures, languages, and knowledge in your community and to incorporate the (hi)stories that comprise your rural school. The main four chapters of this book draw from four principles for rural ML education and are organized as four movements for educators:

The First Movement: Representation and Belonging
The Second Movement: Shared Vision
The Third Movement: Centering Multilingual Learner Families
The Fourth Movement: Collaboration and Community

Each of these movements is centered on people, starting with ML students themselves, and including those who surround MLs: educators, families, and communities. The four principles in this book guide local decision-making for rural educators working with ML students and families. Each of the four principles is important, but together, they form a cohesive ecosystem of support to meet the language, learning, and social developmental conditions for rural MLs to thrive.

Conclusion

This chapter provides an overview of key ideas and concepts that are explored throughout this book and how they can be applied to everyday practice by educators serving rural ML students and families. Demographic data show the growth in the number of MLs across the U.S. in recent years, as well as the disproportionate funding, added costs, and limited professional learning opportunities faced by rural educators who support their MLs. Importantly, rural schools vary, despite sharing the same classification as rural. The variation across rural communities—including the land, the histories of the people, how the community functions, and relationships and social networks that exist within rural communities—matters significantly in the types of programs and services that are available or that you, as a rural educator of ML students, can provide.

Working in rural ML education and with teachers, leaders, counselors, paraeducators, and family liaison staff, I have found a common feature: that rural educators are deeply committed to their students and find creative, local, and innovative solutions to persistent problems of practice. Schools are central and critical spaces for rural identity and community gathering. However, funding constraints, time pressures, technological limitations, geographic and educator isolation, and transportation barriers have made the work of rural educators significantly more demanding than that of their metropolitan counterparts. This has a particularly difficult impact on ML students and families. As rural educators, we require funding and opportunities on par with our metropolitan colleagues in order to begin addressing persistent inequities. This chapter introduced an analogy of four educational "movements" or principles for rural ML education that educators can use to affirm and support learning for rural ML students.

DISCUSSION QUESTIONS FOR CHAPTER 1

1. Reflect on your rural community. What words would you use to describe it? What sounds, images, scents, and feelings does it invoke for you? How is your rural community unique?
2. What strengths can you identify in your rural community? What role do different languages play? Are multiple languages considered a resource or a problem?
3. What do equity and equality mean to you? How would you relate those concepts to rural schools? To ML students?
4. What are "linguistic spaces" as described in this chapter? How does the concept of linguistic spaces relate to schools and classrooms? Do you have examples to draw from?
5. In what ways does the analogy of four movements in a symphony resonate with your work as a rural educator?

2

The First Movement

Representation and Belonging

Maria R. Coady and Cassandra Rubinstein

Introduction

Take a drive to any local rural school and enter the parking lot. Examine your surroundings. What do you see? Are the school's name, signage, and marquee visible? If the marquee is there, is it digital? Does it provide information on school events, such as an upcoming book fair or school holidays? What language is the signage in? What greeting does it display? Identify the entrance of the school. In today's school-safety environment, is the front entrance evident? Is there signage or symbols, such as arrows or instructions, indicating where to go and how to communicate with the entrance staff to enter the doorway? If so, what languages are the instructions in? Where do you go once you pass through the front door? Once inside, what are the immediate material artifacts that you see? Is there family-friendly information and access to school programs, lunches, calendars, and social services in the languages of the families whose children attend the school? Take a closer look at the materials you see, beyond the languages. Do they reflect the social demographics of the

DOI: 10.4324/9781003509875-2

students and families of the school? Do the programs and foods reflect the cultural and ethnic needs and differences of the students that they serve?

Recently, we were speaking with a bilingual Latina undergraduate teacher candidate, Cinthia, who is from a rural farmworker community in North Carolina. Cinthia conveyed how much she truly missed spending time with her family in their small community. As a student studying in the city, Cinthia looked forward to the summer break to return home, eat her mother's home cooking, and enjoy the quiet, slower pace of the countryside. Cinthia went on to describe the sense of belonging that she felt in her rural community back home. Being part of a rural community was integral to Cinthia's identity and belonging. However, she explained that she felt connected to two rural families: her siblings and Spanish-speaking parents, and the sense of family, or *familism*, that she experienced with educators and peers in her school.

Coming from an immigrant home in which her parents spoke only Spanish, Cinthia described how she frequently had to navigate those two spaces. For instance, she translated school information and materials for her parents so that they could keep up with school events and her extracurricular activities. She recounted that when the school administrators called on the phone to provide information on events or to check in, she mediated the conversations by interpreting for her parents. Although one important strength of rural communities is the sense of *familism* and close kin-like relationships that tie people together (Crumb et al., 2022), these strengths aren't the same for multilingual students and families, whose languages and cultures might differ from those of the school (Dean Hughes et al., 2026).

Like rural families that function within rural close-knit communities, Dvořák, our famed composer described in Chapter 1, who composed the first U.S. symphony, *From the New World*, grew up in a low-wealth rural community. His father was a butcher and ran a local inn, and Dvořák was expected to follow in his father's footsteps as the town butcher. However, Dvořák's teacher, Liman, who was the church's choir master, took a keen interest in Dvořák's musical ability and persuaded the family to allow him to pursue music. Dvořák later went to Prague at the age of 16 to study at an organ school.

As a major city that Dvořák had never seen before, Prague was vastly different from his small rural village, even though it was only about 20 kilometers (or 30 miles) away. Dvořák struggled with being different. Unlike the other students, he could not speak German, the main language of communication under the Austrian empire, which was the language of instruction at the school. Dvořák recalled,

> Anybody who wanted to learn anything had to know German. Anyone who knew German well could be dux [leader or composer] of the class, but if he did not know German he could not be dux. My knowledge of German was poor, and even if I knew something I could not get it out. My fellow-pupils looked a little "down their noses" at me and laughed at me behind their backs. And later on they still laughed at me.
>
> *(Dvořák, n.d.)*

Dvořák's sense of self as a minoritized rural young man in a large city undoubtedly had a lasting impact on his work. These moments of struggle and sense of *not* belonging to the group of German-speaking peers shaped Dvořák's commitment to the inclusion of minoritized people. His commitment significantly influenced his compositions, which drew heavily on Czech folk music, and in the U.S., on Black spirituals and Indigenous influences. In other words, Dvořák's strengths derived from his rural upbringing, connection to local folk music and traditions, and cultural and language difference. For Dvořák, music was a tool for self-expression and community representation.

Part I: What It Is

As noted earlier, rural communities and schools are increasingly diverse spaces. The diversity of students attending rural schools cuts across linguistic, racial, ethnic, cultural, socioeconomic, and religious lines. The *representation* of diverse people who participate in rural schools and communities and the 'sense of belonging' that they feel are fundamental to building equity-based schools and practices. In this chapter, we describe what these concepts mean in the context of education and why they are essential to equity-building practices in rural schools and communities for ML students and families. In addition to what these are, in Part II of this chapter, we describe how to implement these ideas and what they look like in practice.

Representation in Schools

Representation of ML students in schools is a dynamic activity—not a "one and done" event—that involves how ML students are identified, acknowledged, positioned, and valued in schools and classrooms. The concept of representation highlights how students' backgrounds such as language and culture are reflected in the material environment of the school. The material environment includes how images, curriculum, and artifacts in the school reflect ML students' identities and knowledge. It also includes how MLs' languages and multilingualism are used and valued in the school environment as normal and everyday practices of communication and learning. In fact, ML students' ability to navigate multiple languages is a *superpoder* or superpower that should be proudly reflected throughout the school environment. Representation further involves school staff, leaders, and teachers who work at the school and who are from similar cultural and linguistic backgrounds to the students that they serve. These key personnel serve as role models for ML students and demonstrate that MLs can take up positions of leadership, agency, and power in rural schools and communities.

Representation of MLs is an ongoing, evolving commitment that must move beyond surface-level recognition. While multicultural events—such as Hispanic Heritage Month (annually in the U.S. from September 15 to October 15), Black History Month, or Asian Pacific American Heritage Month—can serve as important affirming spaces, true representation requires integrating multicultural perspectives throughout the fabric of education. This means embedding diverse histories, languages, and cultural narratives into the curriculum, classroom discussions, and school practices year-round.

Representation involves honoring the multiple identities that ML students carry, recognizing the intersections of language, culture, race, and migration that shape their lived experiences. It demands attention to the cultural wealth these students bring—their bilingualism, worldviews, and community knowledge—and how these can enrich learning spaces for everyone, particularly in rural communities, which are frequently depicted as non-diverse. The representation of groups of people and their contributions to the land we inhabit and to the history of the U.S. is far richer and profound than any single event or month could capture. Representation is a continuous act of inclusion, reflection, and reimagining (Greenwood, 2019) that centers the voices and stories of all people who comprise our country.

Educators have long criticized the superficial "heroes and holidays" approach to multicultural education, a term coined by Christine Sleeter in her early work, which challenges how diversity is reduced to celebratory events focused on famous figures and cultural festivities (Sleeter & Grant, 2008). This critique extends directly to linguistic representation. Confining ML students' languages and cultures to isolated multicultural celebrations, such as a Spanish vocabulary word of the day during Hispanic Heritage Month or a single bulletin board featuring culturally relevant images during designated heritage months, does not constitute authentic representation. Such tokenistic practices can unintentionally reinforce the idea that multilingualism and cultural diversity are special occasions rather than essential, everyday parts of the school community. True linguistic representation, as described in the notion of "in the air, in the halls, and on the walls," requires that students' languages be integrated throughout the daily fabric of instruction, communication, and school life. This means that ML students see their languages in classroom libraries year-round, hear their languages used naturally in academic discussions across content areas, and find their linguistic identities reflected in curriculum materials, assessment practices, and administrative communications consistently, not just during designated heritage celebrations.

Harklau (2000) provides a short definition of student representation in school as "archetypal images of learner identity" that are displayed in the school material artifacts (p. 35). Harklau considers this representation to be non-fixed; rather, it is a dynamic, changing, and negotiated process that continues to evolve over time. In her work with ML students, Harklau challenges the tendency to believe that there is a single image or idea that can capture ML students' identities:

> Representation refers here to the images, archetypes, or even stereotypes of identity with which students are labeled. I argue that representations result from constant attempts to hold a heterogeneous and ever evolving social world still long enough to make sense of it. Whereas identities may be multiple, fragmentary, and subject to constant change, representations are temporary artifacts that serve to stabilize and homogenize images of identities.
>
> *(Harklau, 2000, p. 37)*

Representation of students does not stereotype MLs but instead portrays the multiple identities that show and capture who students are, where they are from, and how they participate in the school and community.

Schools are complex social places that consist of physical and relational spaces and include audible and visual elements. As described in the opening of this chapter, the physical space of the school can be instrumental in creating a welcoming and linguistically affirming environment, where ML students and families' languages are recognized and visible, such as at the front of the school entrance. In contrast, when families or students are not represented in the material culture of the school, the message they receive is that their languages, cultures, and identities are not important to the school community or in its functioning. Nothing could be further from the truth. Research repeatedly and consistently underscores how ML students' first language is a determining factor in their academic achievement and their development of English language and literacy skills (Collier & Thomas, 2017; Cummins, 2000; NCELA, 2023).

Research has shown that minoritized students need educators to be attentive to and deliberate in how they work with diverse students in order to ensure that their students are accurately represented in schools (Landsman & Lewis, 2023; López et al., 2025). Being deliberate about this work is important because minoritized students have historically not been equally represented in educational materials, in the school environment, and across educational programs. This holds true for ML students. In the case of ML students, where there may be a dedicated ESL or language teacher, such as a bilingual educator, MLs can feel more supported than non-ML students. This is because language teachers in ESL or bilingual classrooms aim to create a welcoming, affirming, and representative classroom environment for their ML students (White et al., 2023). Limiting MLs to being represented in ESL or bilingual classrooms, however, is not enough to ensure representation and identity affirmation in the school. Students' multilingual identities must be represented throughout the school, not only in ESL or bilingual classrooms.

At a recent professional development event, we heard bilingual educators describe the need for ML students' languages to be represented "in the air, in the halls, and on the walls." This catchy phrase captures some of the ways in which the representation of ML students can take place. For instance, "in the air" refers to sounds—namely, hearing and speaking—that ML students use. Students' multiple languages should be audible in the school office, hallways, classrooms, library, playground, cafeteria, and so on. The use of students' oral languages sends the message to ML students that their languages matter and, by extension, that they matter. The use of students' first language and hearing it in schools affirms students' identities and multilingual *superpoder*. Students who are not multilingual also benefit from interacting with, hearing, and experiencing multiple languages used in schools and communities and begin to see multilingualism as natural, everyday human communication. As a natural phenomenon, humans are, and can be, bilingual or multilingual, and there are substantial cognitive, social, and economic benefits of bilingualism (Bialystok, 2011, 2021; Spelorzi et al., 2021; Porter et al., 2023; Yow et al., 2024).

Language representation in the physical space of schools and classrooms includes "in the halls and on the walls." ML students acquiring English frequently have strong and well-developed first language oral skills and may be literate in the home language. Those skills are essential to maintain because they provide the foundation upon which students acquire oral English and literacy in English (Escamilla et al., 2022). For instance, ML students can and should continue to read and write in their first language while acquiring literacy in English. This builds MLs' overall linguistic competence.

Research consistently demonstrates the academic benefit of having high levels of literacy in two or more languages (Escamilla, 2022; Escamilla et al., 2014; García et al., 2025). The degree to which MLs' languages are represented in the school's print and material artifacts can reinforce the message of acceptance, the importance of multilingualism, and language and literacy development. Imagine you are a non-English-speaking parent who enters your child's school and classroom and sees their work represented in your home language alongside other material artifacts that capture and affirm the culture of your home. The physical space is an affirmation that creates an environment of welcome, inclusion, acceptance, and care.

Importantly, MLs may speak multiple languages or varieties of language that educators might not realize. ML students' backgrounds are varied and complex linguistically and culturally. They negotiate their multilingual identities in a dynamic process through the exchange of ideas, relationships with peers and adults, language use, literacy, and culture. We have found that many teachers think that their MLs know only one language—most often Spanish in the U.S. However, when we ask the MLs what languages they know, they point to Indigenous languages such as Q'anjob'al, Guaraní, or Otomí, depending on the country and region their families are from. Olszewska (2020) studied the languages and literacies of Chechen refugee background students (RBSs) in Poland. Before working with the four adolescent girls in her study, the educators in the school assumed that the girls were monolingual Chechen speakers who were learning Polish. Olszewska found that the students spoke multiple languages to varying degrees, and all four expressed a desire to use and improve them.

ML students' identities are often more complex than we realize as educators. In another study, DeNicolo (2019) worked with three first-grade girls who attended a Spanish-English bilingual education program called a dual language immersion (DLI) program in the U.S. In DLI programs, students learn academic content and acquire literacy through the use of two languages. The three Guatemalan girls were bilingual speakers of Q'anjob'al, an Indigenous Mayan language spoken in Guatemala and southern Mexico, and Spanish, and were in the process of learning English. Their language identities, which included the use of an Indigenous language at home, were more complex than the girls' teachers had realized. This information is essential for teachers and school staff to serve and communicate with families.

Representation in the Linguistic Landscape

How can teachers and educators in schools represent their ML students' identities and various languages in the school and classroom spaces, and in the material artifacts and culture of the school? Researchers describe the use of multiple languages in the print and semiotic materials of schools and communities as the linguistic landscape (LL). A widely used definition of LL is provided by Gorter (2006), who states that the "linguistic landscape refers to the social context in which more than one language is present. It implies the use in speech or writing of more than one language and thus of multilingualism" (p. 1). Shohamy (2006) expands the definition of the LL to include "everything that can be seen, heard, spoken, and thought. The public space is a negotiated and contested arena that is influenced by a variety of factors and features" (p. 425). LLs are symbolic in that they paint a picture of whose languages are seen and valued, as they are used in signage, in print materials, and in the local environment.

The LL of schools has also been referred to as a "schoolscape" (Gorter, 2018). A schoolscape refers to how languages are (re)presented and used in school spaces. It includes the kinds of visual materials found in schools and classrooms, such as teaching materials and curricula, bulletin and notice boards, and displays of student artwork and essays. In a classroom, labeling objects in multiple languages to support ML student learning is an example of a classroom schoolscape. Bilingual books and materials also contribute to a rich, diverse linguistic schoolscape. These materials demonstrate the "life and communicational needs of the social environment" (Todor, 2014, p. 529). These materials, by virtue of being on display, convey messages to students and families about what languages are important in the school. Because these are subliminal, the languages also convey a hidden curriculum or messaging about what is important to and valued by the school community.

RURAL LINGUISTIC LANDSCAPES

In a study of three *rural* DLI (rDLI) programs that examined the ecosystem of the bilingual programs (such as in the school, town, and community), Coady found that the LL of the community did *not* adequately represent the languages or cultural backgrounds of the people who lived and worked there, despite the fact that multilingual families had labored in the community for more than three decades, working in tobacco fields, construction, and restaurants (Coady et al., 2026). When we spoke with members of local businesses, such as the lead public librarian and director of the community chamber of commerce, they stated that they struggled to include non-English languages and diverse cultures in their print materials, event advertisements, and social services materials because they lacked the resources to translate the materials and did not have strong relationships with bilingual individuals. During our work, we connected these groups with the dual language program principal and staff, and translated materials for them in order to build a more diverse and representative LL and ecosystem where the languages of the people were visible and used. Language representation must be an ongoing, active, and integral part of school and community functioning.

In another study of the LL of one remote rural coastal tourist town, we found that within a period of two decades, more than half of the permanent, year-round residents were Spanish-speakers who initially came to the community directly from Veracruz, Mexico, and later from Honduras. While examining the LL of the tourist town, we noted that visual use of Spanish was virtually absent from the local signage, such as street signs, welcome notices, information brochures, and other material artifacts in the community, such as the community center (Coady & Roberson, 2024). The few representations of Spanish we found were located in the variety store, principally labels on food items, on several health care signs, such as a "no smoking/*no fumar*" sign, and on business cards and solicitations on cork bulletin boards located in the storefront and post office. We noted that the home languages of students were neither visible nor used in the school, church, or community center, places where one would expect diverse people to gather together. We found that the tourist community aimed to retain a monolingual English-speaking image in order to continuously attract patrons who vacationed there. This created a linguistic tension between the language used by people who lived and worked there and the image of the town and tourist industry.

As linguistically diverse people contribute to their local rural communities, their languages should be increasingly visible and reflective of the people who comprise the community. This holds true for schools as well as in small towns and rural public spaces, where representation of students' languages should be in concert with the material artifacts of the school, at extracurricular and family engagement events, and in the processes and procedures of school administration. Our challenge as educators is to remain vigilant of the school environment and how it reflects the linguistic, racial, ethnic, and cultural diversity of the students and families who attend. When students and families are not represented, we can take action to ensure students' linguistic and cultural backgrounds are represented in all aspects of the school, including the curriculum, print materials, signage, media, library resources, websites, and social, health, and mental health services.

Reflect on your own rural community. Who contributes to the functioning and well-being of the community? Is this an agricultural community? If so, are local crops harvested by migrant farmworkers who spend a month harvesting fruit, vegetables, cotton, or tobacco before moving on to the next community? Or does your community house permanent workers in logging, dairy, poultry, or hog processing industries? Are their languages and cultural backgrounds represented in the town, beyond the grocery store where they shop?

Next, take a walk through your local rural town or village. How are the images displayed at the local coffee shop or public library? In what languages are the storefronts and open/closed signs? Are there community events or summer festivals that are announced in English and the diverse languages spoken by community members?

How does representation of ML students' identities (languages, cultures) relate to their sense of belonging? Representation of ML students' linguistic and cultural identities in the school and classroom, both visually and orally, is one way to build students' sense of belonging. Teachers of ML students across all content areas can also identify intentional and strategic ways to use students' first languages in the classroom and throughout the school using translanguaging practices. In the following section, we describe "sense of belonging" and how translanguaging practices contribute to a sense of belonging for MLs and families.

Sense of Belonging

There has been increasing research conducted on the concept of students' "sense of belonging" in schools (Matthews et al., 2024; Qin & Wan, 2015). More than 30 years ago, Goodenow (1993) defined belonging in schools as "students' sense of being accepted, valued, included, and encouraged by others (teacher and peers) in the academic classroom setting and of feeling oneself to be an important part of the life and activity of the class" (p. 25). Adding to that definition, McInerney (2023) described sense of belonging as

> An affective component of a student's feelings of being accepted, valued, included, and encouraged by teachers and peers in the classroom and feeling like an important part of the daily activity of the class.
>
> *(p. 1044)*

Over time, this definition has been further expanded to include concepts of relational trust and care (Bryk & Schneider, 2002; Noddings, 2005), and how students feel connected to their school through their teacher and peer relationships.

An important aspect of this is the role and work of the teacher, and how teachers demonstrate their care for students and their well-being (Noddings, 2005; Roffey, 2013). Matthews and colleagues recently described the concept of sense of belonging as an "historical struggle to have students' intellectual worth recognized, receive cultural affirmation, and obtain high-quality resources for success" (p. 3). This definition adds an historical component to belonging and views a sense of belonging as an act (receive cultural affirmation; obtain resources for success). Thus, a sense of belonging encompasses the historical dimension of diverse people in their communities, a feeling of connection through relationships, the ability and sense of being cared for, and how resources are provided to support growth and success.

For all students, research has shown that there are positive effects of students' sense of belonging on academic achievement, learning, and well-being. The Organisation for Economic Cooperation and Development (OECD) states that a sense of belonging "leads to higher academic achievement, and high academic achievement leads to greater social acceptance and sense of belonging" (OECD, 2017, p. 122). Thus, there is a symbiotic relationship between a sense of belonging, which involves social acceptance and academic achievement. Relationships are key to a sense of belonging. Uslu and Gizir (2017) studied different relationships in schools. They examined teacher-student relationships, student-student relationships, and family involvement. While all of those relationships contributed to an overall sense of belonging, they found that the teacher-student relationship was the most predictive factor leading to a sense of belonging; that is, it had the strongest influence on students' sense of belonging.

There are several pillars of 'sense of belonging' that emerge in the research on how educators can foster a sense of belonging among ML students. These pillars include the following:

- Schools and classrooms are safe, caring, and nurturing spaces;
- Schools and classrooms foster positive relationships between teachers and students, as well as between students;

- ML families are included, informed, and engaged in their child's education in linguistically and culturally responsive ways; and
- Educators understand the concepts of "fitting in" and "standing out" and how they affect students.

(Gray et al., 2018)

While we know that a sense of belonging has strong, positive effects on students' learning and well-being, there is evidence to suggest that this is even more important for ML students and students from minoritized backgrounds (DeNicolo et al., 2017). A sense of belonging is not the same for all students. For students from diverse or vulnerable backgrounds, a sense of belonging operates as a protective factor because it can shield students who are experiencing adversity from the negative effects of those experiences.

McInerney (2023) found five factors that affected ML students' sense of belonging: safety, support networks, language, participation opportunities, and recognition. These five factors are reflected in the aforementioned pillars. McInerney found that teachers have the ability and power to ensure that students' first language is represented and used in the classroom. ML students' sense of belonging doesn't just happen in schools. Teachers play a crucial role in the relationships they build, in how teaching materials and curricula represent the backgrounds—linguistic, racial, and cultural—of the students they teach, and how they continue to reflect on students' experiences. It takes a concerted effort and planning among the teachers, school leadership, and staff to build support networks, safety, and participation. No single educator can (or should) be responsible for ensuring that ML students are represented throughout the school and that they have a sense of belonging.

In the classroom, teachers have a unique platform to create a sense of belonging. For instance, Buchs and Maradan (2021) examined how students' heritage language could be incorporated into cooperative learning strategies in a classroom in a French-speaking region of Switzerland. The existing cooperative learning structures were modified to include ML students' languages, and the teacher provided students with added time to use their heritage languages and to translate text that was brought home and shared with family members. The students were also encouraged to share stories in the heritage language. Teachers in the study described the positive outcomes of the modified cooperative learning strategies on students' cohesion—that is, working together—and a sense of belonging among the ML students in the classroom.

DeNicolo et al. (2024) identified similar outcomes in the U.S. context. Teachers used varied texts that were translated into students' home languages and shared their personal experiences with MLs, which helped build relationships. As in the Buchs and Maradan (2021) study, the teachers had students bring translated text home to use with their families. The impact of this was seen in the relationships with teachers, where MLs believed that their teachers would offer support and help when they needed it. ML students also felt that they were important members of the school and classroom. The authentic relationships that MLs experienced led to an overall sense of belonging in school.

There are other examples from different educational contexts. For instance, in New Zealand, Sutton et al. (2021) examined how teachers built inclusion and a sense of belonging among refugee students. Recognition and valuing of diversity were identified as key features positively contributing to a sense of belonging for those learners. The students reported experiencing greater feelings of inclusion when the school environment acknowledged their diverse backgrounds and multiple cultures.

A sense of belonging builds upon students' cultural backgrounds and affirms their identity. Schools and educators also ensure that there are high-quality curricula, books, teaching and learning materials, and structures in place for students to succeed. The need for linguistic and cultural representation in schools is especially important for students with English language learning needs who have different first or home languages and are racially and culturally diverse. Finally, with a sense of belonging, ML students' intellectual worth and their knowledge of multiple

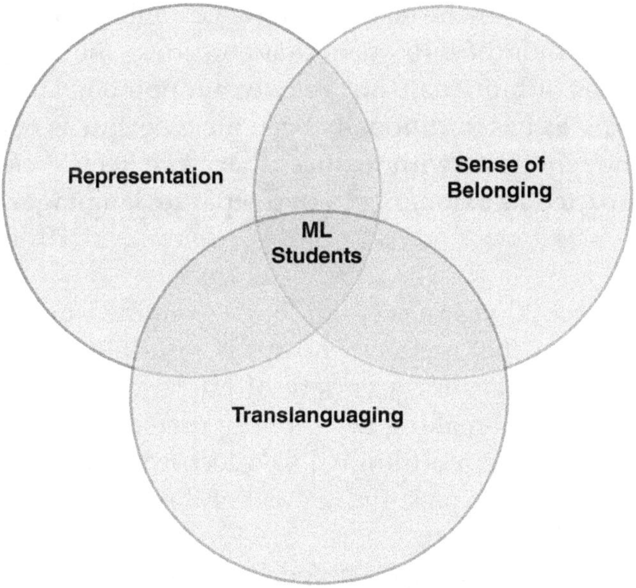

FIGURE 2.1 Intersection of representation, sense of belonging, and translanguaging. Image by the author.

languages and cultural backgrounds are not only recognized but also valued as an important contribution to the school's culture, climate, and functioning. Figure 2.1 displays the intersection of representation, students' sense of belonging, and translanguaging practices.

Translanguaging

Classrooms with ML students can ensure the representation of students, affirm students' identities, and build a sense of belonging through the use of students' first and home languages for communication and pedagogical purposes. The use of students' languages—across their entire linguistic repertoire—can further support learning and literacy development in school. The intentional use of students' various languages in the teaching and learning process, as a fluid language practice, is referred to as translanguaging. According to García and Li, translanguaging is

> an approach to the use of language, bilingualism and the education of bilinguals that considers the language practices of bilinguals not as two autonomous language systems, as has traditionally been the case, but as one linguistic repertoire with features that have been societally constructed as belonging to two separate languages.
>
> *(García & Li, 2014, p. 2)*

Over the past 20 years, scholars have examined how students (and adults, for that matter) who speak multiple languages utilize those languages for a variety of purposes. This process of language decision-making occurs very quickly in the bilingual brain, enabling the multilingual to select from across their languages based on the task, the context of the event, and speakers or other language users.

The idea that different named languages, such as Spanish, French, Haitian, Chinese, and so on, exist in separate boxes in the brain is no longer supported by research in neurolinguistics or the cognitive sciences. In contrast, scholars of language and cognition can isolate the areas of the brain that are stimulated when languages are used orally or in writing. These areas are not separated by language; rather, they exist in a single repertoire from which speakers and language users select. Language speakers and users must adjudicate the languages that they use in a given context and for a specific purpose. For instance, in a classroom of ML students from different linguistic and cultural backgrounds, teachers can plan small group discussions in students' home languages surrounding a particular topic to build background knowledge and sharing. As teachers strategically and purposefully use translanguaging practices based on the students' knowledge of language and of the content, they create spaces in which MLs' languages are resources for learning.

Hamman et al. (2018) describe three guiding principles of translanguaging practices. Principle 1 involves purposeful design and implementation of translanguaging practices by teachers. This principle acknowledges that students benefit from the flexible use of languages in schools and classrooms. The authors describe this principle as "purposeful and strategic" (n.p.) in their instruction. Principle 2 refers to translanguaging practices as a way to promote interaction and inclusion among students. This principle is based on the idea that learning and meaning-making take place when students are engaged, which underscores that learning in one language enhances learning across a student's entire linguistic repertoire. This is because a significant amount of what is learned in one language is transferable or knowable across another language. For example, if an ML student knows how to read and write in their first or home language, then concepts of print, such as directionality of print, punctuation, the alphabetic principle, and so on, have already been learned by the student. These are some of the concepts of print that transfer to English, meaning that ML students do not have to relearn these foundational literacy skills.

Translanguaging practices can support MLs' sense of belonging in classrooms and schools, because students' languages are a significant part of who they are and how they participate in the world.

Imagine for a minute that you are a native English speaker with an emerging knowledge of French, and you are studying in a French-speaking country. Your teacher calls upon you to describe out loud how women obtained the right to vote in the United States so that your peers can learn from you and they can draw parallels between the US suffrage movement and the second wave feminist movement in France in the 1960s. How could you convey your knowledge of that complex historical event? What language strategies would you use? How could you use both English and your emerging knowledge of French to share your knowledge?

Now imagine that you are provided with time and strategic grouping to work in a small group setting with some English-speaking peers. You are encouraged to use your knowledge of English and French to build background knowledge prior to your informal oral presentation. What strategies would you use then? How can your knowledge and use of two languages, with cognates and words with similar roots and meaning, assist you in participating and answering this question?

The more that teachers can model, support, and plan for MLs' learning through the use of their full linguistic repertoire, the more likely students are to engage in learning and skillfully demonstrate what they know and can do. The use of two languages, as in bilingual education and DLI programs, can facilitate ML students' sense of belonging because classroom practices are deeply aligned with the linguistic repertoires of the students. For instance, in a study of three first-grade ML students in a DLI program, DeNicolo (2019) found that translanguaging practices used in the classroom established a sense of belonging among the students. Translanguaging involved purposeful use of students' languages for learning; however, translanguaging in the bilingual program allowed the ML students to connect their home cultures and backgrounds to the school and to use their "funds of knowledge" (Moll et al., 1992). Having access to bilingual education programs and engaging in translanguaging practices created "sites of belonging and security for students" (DeNicolo, 2019, p. 967).

Part II: What It Looks Like

"On the Walls and in the Air"

LANGUAGES IN THE LINGUISTIC LANDSCAPE

Now that we have reviewed three key concepts—representation, sense of belonging, and translanguaging—what these concepts mean, and why they are important steps toward more equitable educational policies and practices in rural schools, let's examine what these look like and how to use them in practice. The figures and images are examples of practices that schools and teachers we have worked with have created to represent a sense of belonging for their rural ML students and families.

One main strength of educators working in rural schools is that they are frequently insiders to their communities and have deep knowledge of how they function. Another main strength is that rural educators wear multiple hats in schools and play multiple roles simultaneously. For instance, a high school Spanish teacher might also be the expert in computer technology for the school and might have the language skills that are used to reach out, translate, and communicate with newcomer families. What this means is that it is not unusual to find a key point person who is responsible for ML students and ML family engagement. However, this can be problematic if the point person leaves the district or school. We strongly encourage that teams of educators collaborate on an ML Plan for students and families. Your school and district plan should include a wide range of programs, processes, and practices that are shared among professionals to ensure representation and a sense of belonging for ML students and families. In other words, all educators are responsible for ML students and can contribute to their success.

Representation

In the aforementioned concept of representation, the physical and material spaces of schools and classrooms must reflect ML students, their cultural and racial backgrounds, and their linguistic *superpoderes*. The languages that they know are assets and strengths—much like the rural concept of familism—that contribute to a thriving community. There are two ways in which representation can be enacted in schools: "I see you" and "you see me." We describe these using visuals and descriptions below.

"I SEE YOU"

The concept of "I see you" refers to the deliberate use and representation of students' languages and cultures in the material environment of the school and in the artifacts, programs, and processes of the school. ML students' and families' cultures and languages should be integrated into all functions and materials in the school. Take stock of what this looks like in your school and classroom. For instance, as noted in the opening of this chapter, what do you immediately notice at the entrance of the school? Or even before that: How and in what languages are families and students represented in the school imagery online?

Ongoing reflection on who is represented and how, and ensuring that students are not stereotyped, is essential to creating a sense of belonging. Outside of the immediate physical space of the school and as schools and districts are increasingly dependent upon the internet to convey school information, student registration, school events, and calendars, how do ML families access this information? Is it in their home languages, and who is represented on the school and district web pages?

We have experienced drawbacks and problems when schools and districts rely on Google Translate and a small translation button at the top of a web page as a way to "work around" the translation and interpretation needs of families. Educators frequently tell us that they have no money for language lines (where interpreters can be called via phone and used in school) or for interpretation services. This is considered best practice in ML education. A consistent source of web error for ML families is that embedded documents on the school website are not translatable by Google. For instance, if your school uploads the weekly or monthly lunch menu or calendar in a PDF document, it will not translate into other languages using web-based tools. In large, nonrural districts, there may be a technology team that works with the district website. However, these staff members might not be knowledgeable about the languages and needs of ML families and students, leaving the website a frustrating experience for them.

In contrast, in small rural communities, because there are fewer staff, educators take on multifaceted roles and tasks. A bilingual paraeducator, teacher, or staff member can work closely with the technology expert to upload materials and to beta-test the district web pages, the school website, the embedded information materials, and translation links. For instance, one school district we worked with moved to a fully online registration process. Even though the technology team believed the materials could be translated into multiple languages using the Google translation button, families had to provide personal information, such as their email, phone number, and address, to first create an account before registering their child. Step two of the process involved checking their email account, clicking on the link, and continuing to upload their child's birth and immunization records.

Unfortunately, when the account link was sent to parents' email, the information defaulted to English text. ML parents could not use the system to register their children because they did not know what the instructions said. What could you do to improve the situation where communication defaults to English and critical materials for ML students are only accessible in English? How can you ensure linguistic representation and support for your ML families who are registering their children in your school? This is indeed a lot to ask in school districts where resources are limited. Yet it illuminates why teams of educators are needed to ensure that MLs are represented in the material artifacts—physical and electronic—used in schools.

Some rural school educators, including principals and teams of teachers, have worked to change their schoolscapes and to represent students' languages. A school that promotes linguistic representation ensures that students and families have access to *all* information, materials, programs, and practices in languages they understand. In many schools today, parents or caregivers may not be print literate. In that case, information must be transmitted orally to parents in languages that they understand. Rural communities may have linguistic assets that schools are not aware of, such as community leaders and business owners who are bilingual and can assist in translation and communication. Linguistic representation leverages the language strengths of rural educators and community members to ensure that the linguistic needs of families and students are met.

Figure 2.2 shows a rural elementary school that displayed information on the marquee, with one side in Spanish and the other in English. As parents drove past the school or dropped off their children in the morning, they learned about school events scheduled for that week. The use of families' home language(s) was a highly successful strategy that not only informed and communicated with families but also fostered a welcoming environment and conveyed a message of inclusion, representation, and belonging.

Bilingual education programs and schools with DLI programs have a distinct advantage over schools that function monolingually. Not only do these programs provide significant learning opportunities and improved academic outcomes for ML students and families, but bilingualism and biliteracy offer cognitive, social, and economic benefits as well. Rural DLI (rDLI) programs are largely understudied. However, some research

FIGURE 2.2 Marquee of rural elementary school with print in Spanish and English. English translation: School closed 15 of April, Food pickup at WMHS every Tuesday and Thursday from 10 to 11 a.m. Image by the author.

is emerging that shows how the rural DLI programs leverage linguistic resources of international teachers while navigating the constraints of metrocentric curricula and conservative community ideologies (Carrillo Carrasquillo et al., 2026; Coady et al., 2026).

Figure 2.3 was taken at a student presentation and family engagement event in a rural Spanish-English DLI program. Second-grade bilingual students participated in a "Wax Museum" or *Museo de Cera* evening event. Both English- and Spanish-speaking families attended the event, and the students spoke about the life of an important figure in either English or Spanish, depending on the language that the visitor selected.

For instance, one second-grade boy described the life of Roberto Clemente, a Puerto Rican professional baseball player. Visitors could "press" a button to choose between English and Spanish (Figure 2.4). Students in this event proudly displayed their knowledge of key figures from diverse backgrounds, while illuminating their oral and written bilingual skills.

Another affirmation "I see you" event was found among the teaching and learning materials of the school. High-quality bilingual books were available for students to select and read.

FIGURE 2.3 Entrance of a "Wax Museum" school event at a DLI school with print in Spanish and English. Image by the author.

Bilingual books and digital texts should be accessible in the school media center and in classroom libraries. Bilingual print materials are useful in the front office and waiting areas of the school where families wait or convene. Bilingual books are not just for students who are print literate in other languages. All students can benefit from seeing and experiencing how different languages are used to convey information in everyday settings.

Some years ago, Coady designed and directed a bilingual home literacy project in rural north central Florida. A Salvadoran family that she worked with had seven children whose ages ranged from 1 to 14 years old. They had recently moved to the rural area when she met them through a school literacy project. While working with the children, my students and she brought bilingual materials and books to the home and read to the children in Spanish and English. Almost instantly, the elementary-grade children opened the books and began counting the words on one page in Spanish and the corresponding number on the opposite page in English.

FIGURE 2.4 Bilingual student presentation with print in Spanish and English at a rural dual language elementary school. Image by the author.

The children, who were emerging bilinguals with some early print literacy knowledge from school in El Salvador, compared the number of words required to convey information in Spanish with the number required to convey the same information in English. This is a prime example of how bilingual children process multiple languages and how they benefit from contrastive linguistics, which involves cross-linguistic comparison. ML students benefit from the opportunities to build their linguistic repertoire. This process of contrastive linguistics increases students' metalinguistic awareness—that is, their awareness of how languages function orally and in print.

Some evidence suggests that, even when there is no direct biliteracy instruction, bilingual students can develop "spontaneous biliteracy" (Coady & Moore, 2010; de la Luz Reyes, 2015)

FIGURE 2.5 Cover of a bilingual book displayed at the entrance of a rural elementary school media center with print in English and Spanish, The Harvest Birds/Los Pájaros de la Cosecha. Image reproduced with permission from the publisher.

by transferring their literacy knowledge across languages. We found that students in our home literacy project developed spontaneous biliteracy in Spanish when they were exposed to and used bilingual books, despite not having ongoing instruction in Spanish. Students transferred what they learned about English literacy, including phonology and phonological awareness, syntax or sentence structure, and writing conventions, into Spanish (Figure 2.5).

"YOU SEE ME"

The concept of "you see me" refers to the ways students' languages and cultures are reflected through the roles, practices, and presence of educators who share similar backgrounds with the students they teach and the families they serve. In rural schools, representation for multilingual learners extends far beyond physical spaces or material artifacts; it is embedded in how educators actively recognize and value students' languages and cultures. Equally important is how multilingual learners and their families see themselves reflected in the educators with whom they interact. For students from diverse linguistic, cultural, and racial backgrounds, access to educators who share aspects of their identities communicates belonging and provides powerful models of possibility.

Rural schools in my state of North Carolina struggle to attract and retain teachers in general and face additional difficulty finding specialized language teachers, such as ESL and bilingual teachers, paraeducators, and core content teachers who are bilingual and biliterate (Coady, 2020; Ruecker, 2021). Teacher attrition and low teacher pay are realities that many rural districts face in the current educational context (Leech et al., 2022). Valuing the languages and cultural knowledge of the bilingual educators and staff in a school district sends a message about whose knowledge matters and how that is leveraged in rural schools to build communities of representation, care, and well-being for ML students. This practice taps into the strengths of rural schools by identifying and utilizing rural networks and kin-like relationships to support MLs.

Recent research has examined the critical role of bilingual paraeducators in rural schools (Oudghiri, 2023; Reeves, 2023). However, scholars are finding that paraeducators are often underestimated for their linguistic and cultural knowledge and strengths. For instance, Reeves (2023) examined the role of bilingual paraeducators in a rural school in Nebraska. In her findings, Reeves detailed the identity work of two Spanish bilingual paraeducators in an elementary school district of a rural, agribusiness company town on the Great Plains. The paraeducators experienced contradictions between the identity positions they wanted to claim—having agency over how they were perceived—and those assigned to them by white monolingual teachers and administrators. This resulted in a source of tension for the paraeducators, who remained undervalued in the schools.

Oudghiri's (2023) year-long narrative inquiry centered on two sisters who were bilingual paraeducators in Ririe, Indiana. The sisters described how they navigated their own immigrant identities while advocating for newcomer multilingual students, by creating a linguistic and cultural "bridge" between the school and families. Oudghiri found that they had deep insider knowledge and awareness of community functioning by how they navigated local practices on behalf of their MLs. She found that

> [a]lthough they felt limited in their impact due to their low status in the school, [the bilingual paraeducators] cared deeply for the emotional, social, and academic well-being of their students, especially the undocumented students. In small, but meaningful ways, the paraeducators saw themselves as a community … [they] amplified the voices of their community by identifying deficit practices that "othered" Latinx students from their classmates.
>
> *(Oudghiri, 2023, p. 120)*

In our work in a rural school district (Coady et al., 2024), we similarly found that bilingual paraeducators' roles were frequently viewed in limiting terms, such as the school's interpreter or translator. Their insider knowledge of the rural community, language and cultural mediation skills, social networking, and advocacy were not fully seen or valued. The bilingual paraeducators in our rural North Carolina study took on the difficult work of outreach for newcomer and immigrant families. One rural paraeducator, Mr. D., described how he felt that the school administration thought he was spending too much time talking with ML families, when in fact he was strategizing with them to identify social and emotional support for their adolescent teenagers who were new to the school. His work also involved identifying health and dental care, transportation, and addressing food insecurity among Latinos in their rural community.

Across these studies in rural America, research shows that rural bilingual paraeducators consistently have to navigate "narrow identity spaces," or the limited ways in which other educators viewed them (Reeves, 2023, p. 70).

Funding from the U.S. Department of Education Title III was formerly meant to target the language learning needs of ML students. Some districts used this funding to hire paraeducators, who are often bilingual and speak the language(s) of the students they serve. Paraeducators are meant to provide supplemental educational support services, but they are not a replacement for a prepared ESL or bilingual-certified teacher. At the same time, paraeducators are given extensive responsibilities for the learning of the ML students, much of which is overlooked, as noted earlier with Mr. D, who provided extensive social and emotional support for newcomer ML families.

In rural schools, identifying the linguistic *superpoderes* and experiences of the bilingual paraeducators is essential. These educators, who have limited access to the same professional development opportunities as their teacher counterparts, need to be included in the overall LL of resources. In addition, all educators in the school and district should be aware of their strengths and contributions, as well as the fact that they are more than the school translator (Figure 2.6).

As rural schools become more linguistically, culturally, and racially diverse, teacher, leader, and staff positions need to reflect and be representative of the students and families who comprise the community. In addition to the need to increase the number of educators with strengths in diversity and multilingual *superpoderes*, these leaders serve as role models for ML students and contribute to an environment of identity affirmation and belonging.

Ms. Zulaika Quintero is the principal of a rural K-8 DLI school in an agricultural community in Florida. A former farm worker and child of migrant parents, Ms. Quintero has been a role model in her leadership position at the school and for the school district. During the COVID pandemic, for example, when schools were closed and most had trouble communicating with their ML families, Quintero reached out to families for regular online meetings to listen to families and provide the services they needed. She

FIGURE 2.6 Welcome to "back to school night" with two bilingual paraeducators at a rural elementary school. Image by the author.

had 95 ML parents regularly attending the online Zoom meetings, a number unheard of by most districts.

Being part of the rural farmworker community was a key factor in her ability to communicate with families. Understanding how migrant agriculture families navigate work and school, and participate in community events, informed the strong relationships she built with families who trusted and confided in her. Quintero described working at the school as "like a second home… my passion" (personal communication, 2021). Director of Charter Programs Juana Brown said about Quintero, "They see themselves in her," Brown said. "She's one of them" (Fradette, 2019, n.p.).

These are several examples of what building representation and a sense of belonging looks like in rural schools with ML students. Rural schools face structural and systemic inequities and challenges, but they also are spaces of familism and care, insider knowledge, and the multiple talents and multifaceted roles of educators. To create equity spaces where ML students and families participate and feel cared for, the languages and cultures of families must be visible and audible in school physical spaces, processes, and procedures. Starting with the entrance to the school and continuing through the school and classroom spaces, walls, and halls, ML students should be recognized and represented.

Educators who work with them need recognition for their own linguistic abilities and cultural knowledge that they regularly use and share. DLI and bilingual education programs utilize multiple languages for instructional purposes; however, all educators can engage in and create learning spaces through translanguaging practices that affirm ML students' identities and that provide ongoing support for their academic learning and English language development.

Conclusion

This chapter introduced the concepts of representation, sense of belonging, and translanguaging, as well as the activities that teachers and educators can engage in to promote and reinforce equitable education for ML students. The main ideas from this chapter include the finding that all students should be represented in the school environment and curriculum, but this is even more important and more complex for ML students who have rich linguistic and cultural backgrounds. Research shows that the more representative the material artifacts, culture, and curriculum are of the students in the school, especially MLs' languages and cultures, the more likely students are to feel affirmed. Affirmation of ML students' identities is a cornerstone of equity and of students' sense of belonging. Students' sense of belonging is predicated on a positive and affirming school environment, strong relationships with teachers and peers, and students' sense that others care about them.

DISCUSSION QUESTIONS FOR CHAPTER 2

1 What does your *school* look and sound like "on the walls" and "in the air"? What languages are present? How is multilingualism represented? How are students' identities represented?
   - Take a walk through the school, beginning in the school parking lot. Note all of the languages you see represented in the material artifacts, including at the front school door and office, hallways, cafeteria, library, and classrooms. How are ML students and families represented? What languages are present or missing? Whose cultures, races, and ethnicities are represented, and do they parallel the demographics of the school?
   - Morning announcements for the school are often made in English only. How can educators add the languages and voices of ML students to the morning announcements? One way to do so is to have two students provide announcements, one in English and an interpreter providing an interpretation into another language.

2 If you are a teacher, what does your *classroom* look and sound like? Are ML students' voices audible? Do they hear and see their languages reflected in announcements, the print environment, anchor charts, and in classroom libraries?

3 All students benefit from being aware of and hearing multiple languages in the school and classroom environment. Take note of these items. How can you increase the number of languages and students' attention to languages around them?

3

The Second Movement

Shared Vision

Introduction

I begin this chapter by departing from the analogy to Antonín Dvořák's life and describe the visionary Jeannette Meyer Thurber, who established the National Conservatory of Music in New York and brought Dvořák to the U.S. Without Thurber's vision for the Conservatory and commitment to inclusive education, Dvořák's *From the New World* American Symphony would not exist.

Mrs. Jeanette Meyers Thurber was born in 1850 and died in 1946 in New York. She was the American-born daughter of a Danish immigrant violinist and was known to be a highly energetic and driven woman (Rubin, 1990). As a young woman, Thurber studied music in Paris at the *Conservatoire de Paris*, though it is unclear what she precisely studied there. After returning to the U.S. from France, Thurber met and married a wealthy New York food merchant and lawyer, Francis Thurber, in 1869. Their combined financial assets enabled the Conservatory's work.

Under the influence and tireless dedication of Jeanette Thurber, the National Conservatory of Music was established in 1885 in New York City. Her inspiration for the American school was the French conservatory system, which provided government financial support to talented students, regardless of gender

DOI: 10.4324/9781003509875-3

or race. Thurber held a similar vision for the American school. Most important was Thurber's vision for the Conservatory. Thurber envisioned a school that was "open to women, people of color, the handicapped, and the poor" (Beckerman, 2003, p. 4). She felt that access to high-quality music education should not depend on a student's ability to pay. Her views and vision were considered highly progressive at the time. Rubin (1990) notes that

> the National Conservatory was the first such institution in the United States to make a special mission of seeking out and encouraging women, minorities, and the handicapped on the basis of talent alone, without charge if the student was unable to pay.
>
> *(p. 296)*

Thurber soon began pursuing Dvořák to move to New York and direct the Conservatory. She, indeed, had a vision for American music, an inclusive educational program, and ensuring a diverse student body. It took Thurber several years and the promise of a large sum of money to convince Dvořák to come to New York. Ultimately, Thurber's vision and financial prompting convinced Dvořák to come to New York in September of 1892. As a Czech composer from humble origins, Dvořák appeared to share Thurber's vision for inclusion and diversity. In fact, she was noted to have gifted Dvořák a copy of Longfellow's *Hiawatha,* the expansive poem that references Indigenous culture and is believed to have influenced some of the music in the *From the New World* symphony (Beckerman, 2003, p. xx).

Part I: What It Is

Shared Vision in Education

This story reveals that individuals may hold a vision or image of the future for an organization, but it takes a group of people, or a team of educators, to negotiate and implement that vision. A shared vision among educators is like a collective north star that keeps the group progressing in the same direction and working toward the same goals. This involves a future image of the school that reflects what educators collectively want their school to look like. A shared vision can unify educators around a common purpose (Wang & Rafiq, 2009). However, developing and implementing a shared vision is challenging because the concept can initially seem abstract or overly theoretical (Murphy & Torre, 2014).

Peter Senge (1990) defines a shared vision as an organization's ability to hold a "shared picture of the future it seeks to create" (p. 9). Senge's book, *The Fifth Discipline*, argues that successful organizations act as *learning organizations*, meaning they continually build their capacity to adapt, grow, and improve. He introduces five "disciplines" that make this possible, one of which is a shared vision.

Shared vision work is closely linked to organizational learning, as it shapes how knowledge is created and disseminated within the school. In schools, this means generating a collectively developed view of what the community wants to become. Developing a shared vision involves asking what educators hope to create together and how they want their school to work (DuFour & Eaker, 1998; Senge et al., 2012). As Pekarsky (2007) emphasizes, a vision must be more than a slogan; it should guide the daily work of educators and the rhythms of school life. When implemented well, a vision moves beyond theory and becomes a practical tool for guiding decisions and shaping schoolwide practices (Hord, 1997).

In their book, *Schools That Learn*, Senge et al. (2012) describe five approaches to developing a school vision, each reflecting a different balance of leadership direction and community or educator involvement. *Telling* and *selling* are the most leader-centered approaches: telling involves simply announcing the vision, while selling adds persuasion to gain support. These ideas can be useful when a school faces urgent challenges that require quick decision-making, but they struggle to build deep commitment because teachers, staff, and families have little ownership over the outcome. *Testing*, Senge's third approach, represents a middle ground in which leaders present a draft vision and gather feedback before finalizing it, allowing staff perspectives to shape the final direction if leaders genuinely incorporate their input.

More collaborative approaches include *consulting* and *co-creating*. Consulting begins with collecting ideas and experiences from teachers and other stakeholders such as counselors, paraeducators, staff, parents, and partners, which leaders then synthesize into a shared vision. This method builds trust because educators see their contributions reflected in the direction of the school. Co-creation goes further by directly involving educators, families, and community members in the full visioning process through dialogue, reflection, and collective decision-making. Although more time-intensive, the co-creation process of developing a shared vision yields the strongest sense of purpose because the vision emerges from the community itself rather than from a single individual presenting it to others.

Together, these five approaches highlight that developing a meaningful school vision is not just a technical task but a relational one, a dimension of rural ML education that is discussed in greater detail in the following chapters. The more a school involves educators in the process, the more likely the resulting vision will guide daily practice, strengthen the learning community, and support long-term change. Developing a shared vision, therefore, requires collaboration, reflection, and knowledge exchange (Huffman, 2003). When educators articulate a shared picture of the future they hope to create, they provide direction for learning, decision-making, and growth across the community (Senge, 1990).

A significant amount of research on vision work focuses on school leadership. Principals are often viewed as central to promoting and sustaining a shared vision (Mitchell & Sackney, 2006; Murphy et al., 2009), though their influence may be shaped by the school's unique context (Barnett & McCormick, 2003). Principals play a key role in understanding the needs and climate of the school community (Stolp & Smith, 1995). Research on dual language immersion (DLI) bilingual education programs shows that principals can act as 'linchpins' and play critical roles in the direction and sustainment of programs (Menken & Solorza, 2015). In my work with rural DLI (rDLI) programs,

I have found that principals fill similar roles but also navigate resource constraints such as access to bilingual teachers and curricula, and geographic and social isolation. While the importance of shared vision in school development is well documented (Harris & Jones, 2010; Huffman, 2003; Murphy & Torre, 2014; Pekarsky, 2007), less is known about how collaboratively created vision supports the development of diverse school communities that cross-cultural or linguistic boundaries, or that span across schools, such as elementary to high school levels.

Shared Vision for Rural MLs

A shared vision for educators working with rural MLs involves a jointly built understanding of what success looks like for rural multilingual learners (ML) students and is shaped by several important factors:

- the realities of rural communities, their history, how they function, and the knowledge held in the community;
- the linguistic and cultural assets that ML students bring to their communities and into the school environment;
- the resources (or limited resources) that schools have, which are particularly pertinent to rural schools; and
- the long-term outcomes that educators seek for all students, families, and the community, including high levels of bilingualism and biliteracy, deep cultural understanding across groups, academic success, and social well-being.

Educators who have a shared vision for rural MLs know who the ML students are, what they need, what their strengths are, including linguistic and cultural strengths, and what they are collectively committed to doing on behalf of MLs and their families. This means working beyond the insulated groups, such as the ESL team, bilingual family liaison staff, or ML administrators, to include *all* educators who work with ML students and families.

The experiences of MLs in schools vary widely, and a shared schoolwide vision among educators' approaches to MLs can make a significant difference. As a teacher and researcher, I have observed practices ranging from classrooms where ML students are left isolated at the back of the room, unattended in their learning, and unable to complete tasks, to situations where MLs' languages and cultural backgrounds are uplifted by teachers as "experts" in the room, highlighting their unique linguistic and cultural knowledge. In a rural classroom with a highly prepared English language arts (ELA) teacher who taught ESL through ELA, the teacher's deep knowledge of his students' backgrounds and home countries was evident and impressive. He prepared a lesson on cultural monuments and had students present important monuments from their home countries. They did this using English and their home language. He then engaged students in contrasting the monuments by situating them in a historical timeline.

A shared vision for rural MLs among educators centers on a common understanding of the assets MLs bring to schools and a shared recognition that linguistic and cultural diversity strengthens rural communities. In this vision, there are four key ideas: first, educators collaborate across disciplines and grade levels to ensure that MLs are fully included in academic, social, and extracurricular life. Second, a shared vision among educators emphasizes high expectations, supported by culturally and linguistically responsive teaching, that values students' home languages and community knowledge as vital components of learning.

Third, teachers, administrators, and families work together to create environments where multilingualism is celebrated and sustained, not merely accommodated or—worse—ignored or eliminated. Finally, a shared vision also calls for systemic supports—professional development, resource allocation, and policy advocacy—that reflect the conviction that every student, regardless of language background or zip code, deserves access to rigorous, affirming, and inclusive education that prepares them to thrive locally and globally. This chapter emphasizes the classroom- and school-based practices that educators engage in, together, to support the learning and well-being of ML students.

I've seen how powerful it can be when rural educators of MLs come together to learn, reflect, and problem-solve, identifying solutions to the challenges MLs face. One example comes from Levy County, Florida—a small, agricultural community in the north-central region of the state. Families in that community work on peanut fields, in hay production, and in palm tree nurseries, surrounded by stretches of farmland and long country roads that separate the towns. The landscape itself shapes education: the district comprises four main townships, and the distances between them make collaboration among educators across schools difficult.

Over a period of three years, a group of rural ML educators participated in a professional development (PD) program, Project STELLAR (Supporting Teachers of English Language Learners Across Rural Settings). The program began with online coursework supported by synchronous online meetings. Within a very short period, the educators began to form relationships and share their experiences as members of the rural community, drawing on diverse backgrounds. They established a collective culture of relational trust (Bryk & Schneider, 2002). In fact, they learned a great deal about each other in a safe and democratic space.

In the first semester of the program, the educators indicated in their feedback forms that they preferred in-person meetings. The in-person meetings required that program educators travel long distances to meet. However, the appeal of meeting in person with a shared purpose or vision and trust mattered significantly to them. We modified the PD project to accommodate teachers' and educators' schedules and to rotate in-person meetings across three main towns to reduce the burden of driving for any participant. Out of these efforts to be together and create a shared vision grew something remarkable—a sense of *synergy*, or fuel, that changed how they saw themselves and their work.

As teachers reflected on their ML students, their challenges, and their local realities, their combined energy sparked new ideas and motivation. One teacher described how collaboration replaced the sense of isolation that often comes with rural teaching, where "you wait for administration to make decisions" and "just do your best to follow." Working together made them feel capable of creating change rather than waiting for it. Another educator, Adela, put it best:

> It is like fuel. The time I get to spend with a colleague is revitalizing. It's not about gossip—it's about having a partner who shares your vision. When you both believe in something, you know it will get done. One will support the other.

That shared energy—rooted in trust, democratic relationships, group and individual reflection, and a shared vision for the success of their multilingual learners—became the group's heartbeat. Even informal conversations grew into professional learning opportunities. Through structured sessions and spontaneous exchanges, educators began to build their own *place-conscious expertise*: knowledge grounded in their rural realities, and a shared vision for ML students and families in their local communities.

What are the characteristics of a shared vision? Earlier, I mentioned four key concepts that undergird a shared vision among rural educators of MLs: collaboration across disciplines and grades, shared high expectations, educators and families working together to celebrate multilingualism, and systemic supports for MLs. To summarize, these concepts include:

1. **Collaboration across disciplines and grade levels** to ensure that ML are fully included in academic, social, and extracurricular life.
2. Educators emphasize **high expectations**, supported by culturally and linguistically responsive teaching, which values students' home languages and community knowledge as vital components of learning.
3. Teachers, administrators, and families **work together** to create environments where multilingualism is celebrated and sustained.
4. **Systemic supports** for MLs that reflect the conviction that every student, regardless of language background or area, deserves access to rigorous, affirming, and inclusive education that prepares them to thrive locally and globally.

These four concepts work together beyond the classroom level with individual teachers and, instead, bring educators together as collaborators and co-creators of school-level programs and approaches for ML students.

Part II: What It Looks Like

A shared vision becomes truly meaningful when it takes shape in the everyday practices, relationships, and decisions of rural educators. Part I of this chapter provides the conceptual and theoretical foundation for shared vision. This section moves toward application: what shared vision looks like when rural educators collaborate, act collectively, and build coherence around the successes of MLs. In rural communities, where distances, limited staffing, and sociopolitical histories shape the contours of schooling, a shared vision emerges both through intentional professional structures and through community-based ways of knowing. In fact, in my prior work in rural Florida, the educators' shared vision was evident long before it was implemented. We began with educators talking about MLs and who they are, making decisions about language development instruction, articulating their (mis)conceptions of immigrant or migrant families, and then working across grade levels and even schools to ensure continuity of learning.

The following sections elaborate on the concepts introduced in Part I and on scholarship on rurality, multilingualism, organizational learning, and equity-oriented leadership. Shared vision is not a slogan but a dynamic, negotiated, participatory, and deeply relational set of commitments enacted by rural educators in their schools and communities.

Bilingualism and Biculturalism as Assets: The Foundational Element of Shared Vision for MLs

The first visible hallmark of shared vision for rural MLs is an asset-based orientation toward students' bilingualism and biculturalism. Educators who share a vision intentionally counter deficit narratives, particularly those that position rurality itself as a deficit space or that portray ML students as lacking English proficiency, academic readiness, or cultural belonging (Coady, 2019; Coady & Escamilla, 2005). Consider what people outside your community think about rurality. The mainstream media continues to paint rurality as backward, under-resourced, in decline, and white and monolingual (John & Ford, 2017). The reality is far from that. Rural assets, including multilingualism, are present throughout rural communities and provide a foundation for reversing deficit views.

In rural districts across Florida, my colleagues and I found that teachers with a strong shared vision consistently described MLs' bilingualism as a *community resource*, not a challenge to be overcome (Coady et al., 2023b). Their language echoed the notion that multilingual students enhance rural economies, civic life, and cultural vitality. For example, educators in agricultural communities recognized the sophisticated biliteracies many migrant students develop through cross-border schooling, remittances, and multilingual family communication. In a project described earlier, *Libros de Familia* (Family Books), we found that access to bilingual books fostered spontaneous biliteracy among students and their parents. These added assets, such as language resources and home literacy practices, were key to improving literacy and reading for MLs. This aligns with Yosso's (2005) concept of community cultural wealth, which broader coalitions of educators have increasingly adopted.

When an asset-based stance becomes collectively held through shared articulation and vision, it influences not only classroom practice but also staffing decisions, scheduling, assessment, and community engagement. Teachers begin asking not, "How do we help these students catch up?", but rather, "How do we make sure their linguistic and cultural strengths are central to learning?" In rural DLI (rDLI) programs (Coady et al., 2026), principals have described their hiring practices for bilingual and multilingual teachers, whereby they will not hire teachers or staff who do not share a vision of language-as-resource (Ruiz, 1984) among their ML students.

Because rural educators often work in small, tightly woven communities, when shared vision takes root, educators start to articulate the ways MLs sustain rural life through labor, language, cultural contributions, and community participation. We documented this phenomenon in rural northern Florida, where immigrant families bolstered local economies facing population decline (Coady et al., 2020). Recognizing these contributions reshaped teachers' beliefs, transforming policy discussions and instructional decisions. Holding an asset orientation is not merely a belief; it is the first necessary building block for a shared vision and one that requires collective learning, trust, and reframing.

Opening in-person or online spaces for rural educators to meet and discuss MLs and their families, the assets they bring, and the contributions they make can occur within professional learning settings. I have created spaces in rural communities with bilingual paraeducators, teachers, school counselors, and administrators. Some groups, such as bilingual paraeducators, were organized by background and preparation, whereas others were organized for learning by degree program and interest areas. Identifying like-minded colleagues who want to learn more about their MLs and how to improve instruction and relationships is an important step, followed by establishing consistent spaces for educators to meet and develop a shared vision for rural MLs.

Valuing Diverse Cultural and Linguistic Knowledge as Central to Learning

A second key component of shared vision is educators' willingness to treat linguistic and cultural knowledge as diverse, dynamic, and essential to academic development. Teachers in rural communities often have deep local knowledge of place, community histories, and rural livelihoods. ML students bring equally valuable knowledge that may be less visible in schools but is no less important. For example, during Project STELLAR, teachers frequently used their Professional Learning Community (PLC) time to explore how students' cultural and linguistic repertoires could anchor instruction. This included

- designing content units that draw on place-based or agricultural knowledge, as well as cross-cultural migration stories;
- integrating translanguaging practices that allowed students to utilize their full linguistic repertoires and expand their repertoires (García & Li, 2014; Hamman-Ortiz, 2024); and
- recognizing students' roles as linguistic brokers within their families and in their communities.

Through these efforts, educators cultivated what Gruenewald (2003) describes as critical place-based pedagogy or *place-conscious teaching*, which situates learning within the historical, cultural, and economic realities of rural contexts (see also Greenwood, 2019). Teachers in the STELLAR project repeatedly emphasized how learning from one another deepened their understanding of ML student assets. Their shared vision emerged not from directives but from collective inquiry, collaborative problem-solving, and trust-building—elements central to organizational learning (Huffman, 2003; Senge, 1990).

Another way shared vision can be leveraged is through articulation plans for ML students who transition within schools and for MLs transitioning to new schools, such as advancing from elementary to middle school. Levy County, Florida, teachers, counselors, and ESOL specialists collaboratively developed articulation plans for ML students transitioning from elementary to middle and middle to high school. The plans included the MLs' identities, learning styles, and accomplishments, notes on how best to communicate with families, and any additional documentation to inform the MLs' new teachers in building relationships with them and facilitating their learning. Specifically, the transitions—often difficult in rural districts due to geographic distance, small staff, or inconsistent programming—became smoother when educators shared this information with each other.

This practice is consistent with the literature on shared vision and schoolwide coherence, which emphasizes continuity of vision across grade bands as essential for student success

(Mitchell & Sackney, 2006; Murphy & Torre, 2014). As noted elsewhere, Bryk and Schneider's (2002) seminal work on relational trust finds that trust is the core mechanism enabling school improvement. In Project STELLAR, relational trust emerged among educators from geographically distant rural schools who committed to in-person meetings despite long travel times. This trust fueled collective risk-taking, experimentation with bilingual strategies, and advocacy for systemic changes within the district.

Finally, rural educators, as a group of professionals engaged in learning and operating as a learning community, can participate in reflection cycles that identify persistent challenges faced by MLs, gather community-based perspectives, and collaborate with families and colleagues to address them. As rural educators work together and share their professional experiences, they test and disseminate new strategies in classrooms while refining shared practices through collective dialogue. The ideas generated when one moves from discussing MLs and creating a shared vision to implementing practices that support MLs while upholding their languages and cultures are promising. The key to successfully moving from talking to implementation is creating a consistent, shared time and space where rural educators can convene, reflect, engage in dialogue, and challenge deficit perspectives.

Recognizing ML Families as Contributors to School and Community Well-Being

Shared vision also manifests in how schools position ML families—not as outsiders but as essential contributors to rural community life, functioning, and thriving. One question I frequently ask is, for whom is this rural community thriving? If the answer does not include immigrant and ML families, then it is likely not thriving for everyone. Across the states where I have worked in rural teacher preparation, teachers consistently describe ML families as central to community development, local economies, cultural vibrancy, and school engagement. However, rural ML families are too often framed as "hard to reach" or, worse, framed as being uninvolved in their child's education, due to language barriers or work schedules (Coady et al., 2015). Shared vision reframes the issue: it asks what systemic and linguistic supports the school must establish to reach *them*. When educators adopt this stance together, family engagement transforms.

- Meetings are held at times convenient for farmworkers.
- Interpretation is provided not only for formal events but also for informal conversations.
- Materials are translated proactively rather than reactively.
- Families become co-educators and co-designers of learning activities.

Meaningful family engagement in rural communities occurs when districts acknowledge the central role of ML families in sustaining rural schools (Reeves, 2023). One successful example came from a rural Florida district where the superintendent held monthly *Coffee with the Superintendent* sessions. These were times when families could engage with the district superintendent and leaders and share stories and the district vision for all students. When implemented with cultural responsiveness, such gatherings can operate as relational spaces that redistribute power from top-down to horizontal sharing. Families help identify issues, articulate concerns, and shape district policy. These meetings create trust, deepen school-community relationships, and reveal the cultural and linguistic expertise that families bring. Shared vision compels educators to bridge the knowledge- and identity-based gaps between school and home. Instead of assuming that school norms represent "neutral" or universal ways of knowing, educators recognize that ML homes hold rich cultural, linguistic, and relational knowledge that is equally important.

Participatory methods, in which educators work with families to identify problems and solutions, enable schools to move from consulting families to co-creating approaches that support ML students. In rural areas, participatory approaches are particularly powerful because they challenge hierarchical structures that often exclude marginalized communities, draw on the collective wisdom and lived experience of ML families, and support equity-oriented organizational learning. This mirrors action-research models often used in rural school improvement efforts (Azano & Stewart, 2016).

Leverage Assets through CoLABs: A Shared Vision for Community-Based Innovation

The CoLABs model developed by Bess de Farber et al. (2017) offers a deliberate and highly structured process through which communities can surface shared strengths, clarify needs, and co-design solutions grounded in collective assets. Rather than centering deficits or isolating individual challenges, CoLABs create a facilitated space where participants articulate what they can contribute and what they hope to achieve. In rural multilingual learner contexts, this shift is crucial. Educators often contend with narratives that frame rurality as lacking resources or expertise, yet the CoLABs process makes visible the rich knowledge, relationships, and cultural assets that already exist within a community.

To initiate a CoLAB, a facilitator creates a card containing core information that participants complete before the CoLAB begins. A sample CoLAB card is shown in Figure 3.1. Participants use cards to share information during three-minute exchange sessions, or "rounds." Participants have about 30 seconds to find a partner with whom they will share information. First, the pair quietly reads the information on their partner's card. Then they can have a brief conversation about something that interests them (Figure 3.2). The CoLAB is a process by which a group can map its assets and generate collaborative possibilities. In a debrief session, participants engage in turn-taking, documentation, and reflection so that all voices contribute to the emerging vision. The process concludes with a concrete, co-created plan for following up on the group's shared assets and resources, and feasible next steps. More about the CoLAB can be found in de Farber's book, *Collaborating with Strangers: Facilitating Workshops in Libraries, Classes, and Nonprofits*.

Educators who wish to participate in a CoLAB can begin by cultivating conditions for trust and transparency. This involves setting norms for participation, clarifying the purpose of the gathering, and ensuring that MLs and their families are positioned as contributors rather than recipients. Tools such as asset-mapping protocols, structured dialogue prompts, and visual recording techniques help maintain focus and keep the group oriented toward collective problem-solving. Even in small rural

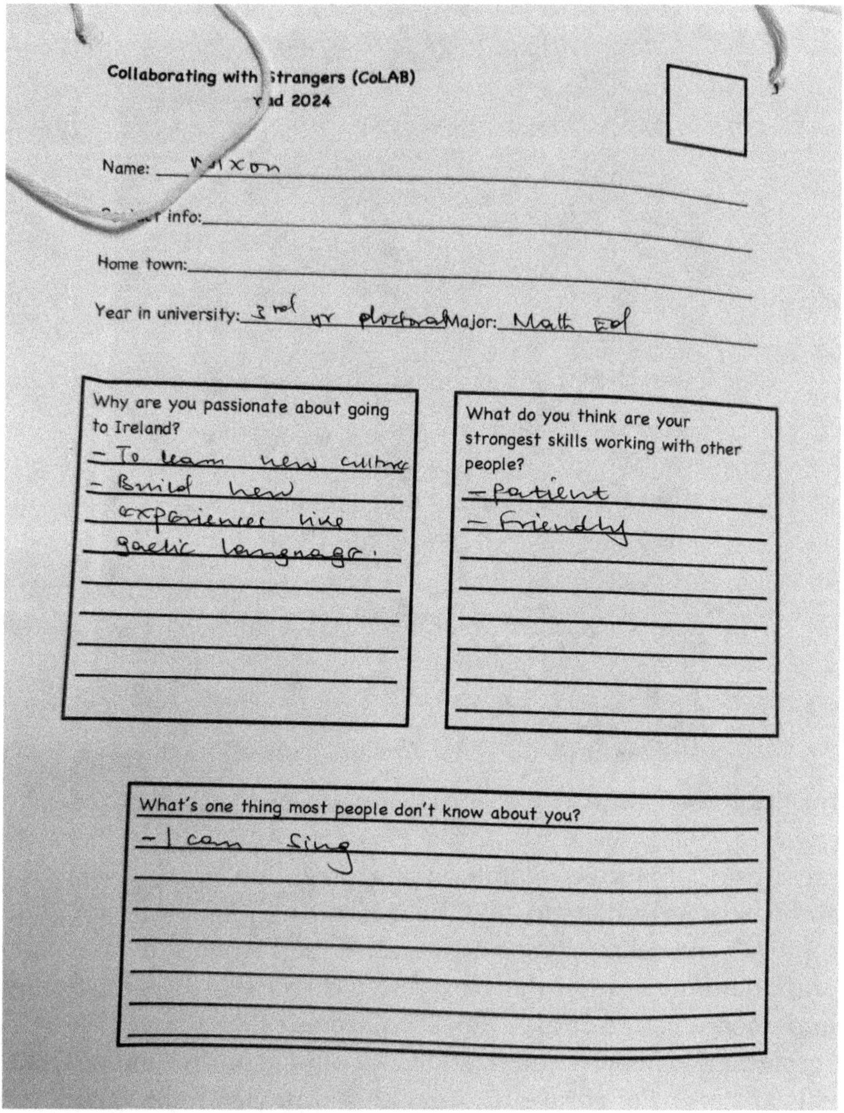

FIGURE 3.1 Sample CoLAB card from rural educator event. Image by the author.

districts with limited staffing, a well-designed CoLAB can be conducted in a single session or across multiple shorter meetings, depending on the community's needs.

When used effectively, CoLABs become more than a planning exercise. They provide educators with a tool for building

FIGURE 3.2 Participants in a CoLAB event for rural educators. Image by the author.

cross-role alliances, counteracting isolation, and sustaining shared commitments to MLs. The resulting plans reflect a community's authentic priorities, because they emerge from collaborative inquiry rather than top-down directives. These activities underscore Senge et al.'s (2012) argument that shared vision is strengthened when organizations recognize and mobilize internal expertise. For rural educators, this approach reinforces a narrative of possibility: that meaningful, locally responsive change is not only achievable but also strengthened by the community's diversity and interconnectedness.

Practices That Result from Shared Vision

When a shared vision is truly internalized across a rural school system, it becomes visible through concrete practices. These include having educators work in strategic cross-disciplinary meetings, developing and sharing ML student profiles, taking instructional risks and leadership actions to support first-language development, pooling rural resources, and building school environments that celebrate multilingualism.

Strategic Cross-Disciplinary Meetings

One of the most visible expressions of a shared vision is the presence of purposeful, recurring cross-disciplinary meetings. These are not perfunctory check-ins but structured times when ESL (or ESOL) language specialists, classroom teachers, administrators, counselors, interventionists, and paraeducators gather to analyze student progress and co-plan instruction. This model echoes the PLC structures described by DuFour and Eaker (1998), but in rural multilingual contexts, the approach takes on added significance. The meetings serve as a hub where each educator's expertise is pooled, teachers who often work in isolation gain access to colleagues' insights, and ML student needs are addressed collectively rather than left to individual teachers.

Participants in these meetings engage in practices such as reviewing recent work samples, analyzing classroom observations, examining language proficiency data and the corresponding instructional practices that will impact student learning and development, and identifying areas where students need added targeted support. For instance, educators convene to collectively review and interpret English language proficiency scores for their ML students. The meetings extend beyond data analysis, however. Educators intentionally leverage one another's strengths: the ESL specialist's deep knowledge of language acquisition; the content teacher's understanding of disciplinary literacy, such as mathematics, science, and ELA; the counselor's awareness of social-emotional dynamics; and the administrator's perspective on policy and scheduling constraints. This asset-sharing creates a dynamic, strengths-forward culture in which educators recognize that no single role holds all the answers. In rural communities, where staff may carry multiple responsibilities, this recognition is essential.

Strategic cross-disciplinary meetings also support critical transition planning for MLs. As students transition from elementary to middle school or from middle to high school, educators collaborate to ensure continuity through articulation planning, as described earlier. They discuss each student's language profile, instructional history, and strengths. They highlight successful accommodations, preferred learning environments, and family insights that should travel with the student. These conversations disrupt the typical rural pattern in which student histories vanish during transitions due to staff turnover or limited record-keeping systems. Instead, intentional articulation ensures that incoming teachers begin with a nuanced understanding of each learner, allowing for more seamless academic and linguistic support.

ML Student Profiles

Another concrete practice that emerges from a shared vision is the creation of multilingual learner profiles that follow students from year to year. These profiles, developed collaboratively and refined over time, function as living documents that capture students' linguistic strengths, cultural assets, interests, preferred scaffolds, and academic progress. In our work with rural educators, we created student profiles through informal interviews with high school students. The idea spread from high school teachers to other grade levels when educators recognized the benefit of the profiles to inform their work. Rather than relying solely on formal assessments, educators use multiple sources: classroom observations, student interviews, family input, and portfolio artifacts. The profiles shift the narrative from deficit-focused progress reports to strength-based portraits of learners. An example is Figure 3.3.

In rural school systems, where staffing turnover may be frequent and ESL specialists serve multiple schools, these profiles are indispensable. They prevent the annual "reset" that MLs often experience when they encounter new teachers who are unfamiliar with their backgrounds and histories. A well-designed profile communicates essential information to any educator who will support the student, ensuring greater continuity and reducing instructional fragmentation. When shared across teams and embedded into PLC discussions, the profiles

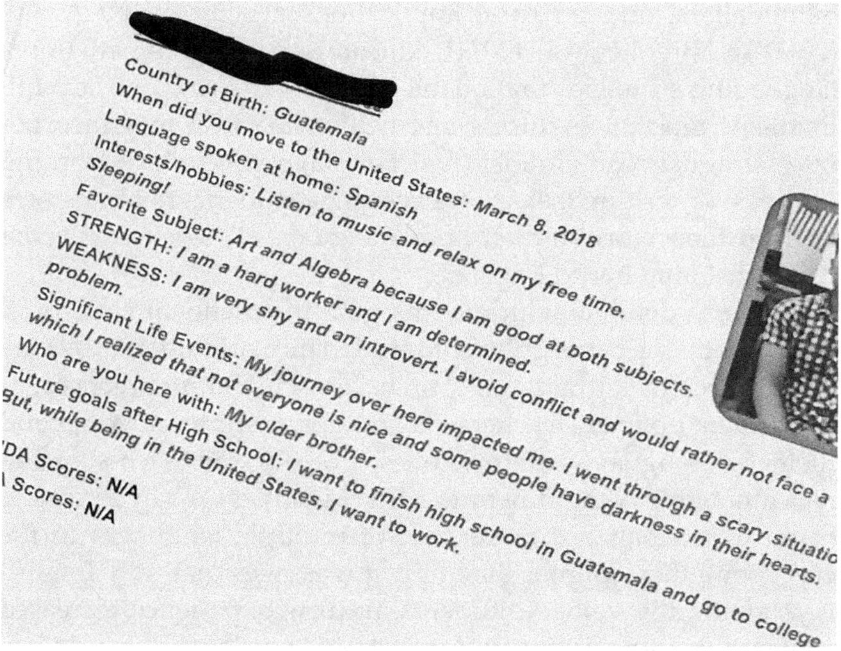

[redacted]
Country of Birth: Guatemala
When did you move to the United States: March 8, 2018
Language spoken at home: Spanish
Interests/hobbies: Listen to music and relax on my free time.
Sleeping!
Favorite Subject: Art and Algebra because I am good at both subjects.
STRENGTH: I am a hard worker and I am determined.
WEAKNESS: I am very shy and an introvert. I avoid conflict and would rather not face a problem.
Significant Life Events: My journey over here impacted me. I went through a scary situatio which I realized that not everyone is nice and some people have darkness in their hearts.
Who are you here with: My older brother.
Future goals after High School: I want to finish high school in Guatemala and go to college ut, while being in the United States, I want to work.
DA Scores: N/A
Scores: N/A

FIGURE 3.3 Teacher-created multilingual learner profile. Image by the author.

help educators co-plan instruction that honors students' identities and previously demonstrated competencies.

Moreover, the act of educators co-developing profiles fosters deeper relationships between teachers, students, and families. Educators engage families as partners in describing the child's linguistic and cultural background, home literacy practices, and aspirations. This collaboration strengthens trust and positions families as essential contributors to the school community. As profiles circulate between teachers and across years, they serve as artifacts of collective commitment, evidence that the shared vision is not theoretical but enacted.

Supporting First-Language Development

A shared vision also emboldens educators to take instructional and programmatic risks that affirm students' first languages. These risks are principled, research-aligned actions rooted in the understanding that bilingualism is an asset. Drawing on scholarship by Escamilla et al. (2014) on fostering biliteracy and bilingualism, and on rural applications articulated by Azano (2011) and Brenner et al. (2021), educators experiment with translanguaging strategies that enable students to draw on their full linguistic repertoires during instruction. Teachers may incorporate bilingual read-alouds, dual language vocabulary learning routines, or writing tasks that encourage students to brainstorm or draft their work in their home languages before transferring and translating it into English.

In rural districts with monolingual instructional structures, such risk-taking can require bold leadership. Administrators may need to reconsider materials purchases, scheduling practices, or assessment policies. Teachers may need support to move beyond their own language comfort zones (Li, 2020). Yet each step signals a tangible commitment to MLs' identities. When educators begin to normalize the presence of multiple languages in the classroom, they counter the implicit messages that only English is academically valued. Students, in turn, experience increased confidence, engagement, and investment.

These risks also inspire broader cultural shifts. When rural teachers experiment openly with new practices, they model a growth mindset for colleagues. When rural administrators publicly endorse first-language development, they tap into the rural community strength of innovation (Crumb et al., 2022). Over time, risk-taking becomes a collective habit rather than the isolated action of a single educator, underscoring how rural communities function nimbly and flexibly through innovation and ingenuity. In this way, the shared vision becomes self-reinforcing, fueling further changes that benefit MLs.

Across-School Resourcing

As noted earlier, rural schools often face wide disparities in staffing levels, available materials, and access to PD. A shared vision encourages districts to adopt a systems approach by pooling resources rather than allowing each school to struggle independently. This pooling can take many forms: sharing instructional materials, jointly funding bilingual resources, coordinating schedules so ESL specialists can serve multiple school campuses more effectively, or creating district-wide professional learning cohorts. Professional learning cohorts have been highly successful among rural educators, either in person or online. The work of teacher educators and the WIDA consortium under Project RESPECT (Rural Educators Self-Reflecting and Practicing Equity-Centered Teaching for English Learners) demonstrates how a successful cohort of rural educators comes together to share professional learning online (Luxemburg-Casco Schools, 2024). That work has led to educator collaboration and presentations at national conferences (Cranley et al., 2025), see Figure 3.4.

Partnerships with universities and regional organizations play a crucial role in this process. Sustainable PD in rural areas requires long-term relationships, not isolated workshops. Through partnerships, rural educators gain access to research-based strategies, coaching, and collaborative inquiry cycles. University faculty and graduate students can help facilitate CoLABs, lead study groups, or support teacher action research. The reciprocity of these partnerships strengthens the district's overall capacity and ensures that rural educators are not left to navigate multilingual education challenges on their own.

FIGURE 3.4 National education conference with rural educators. Image by the author.

Pooling resources also builds social capital within the district. Teachers who previously felt isolated discover professional allies across campuses. Administrators recognize that their challenges are shared and that solutions can be co-designed. Ultimately, the district becomes more adaptive and resilient by operating as an interconnected system rather than as a collection of disconnected schools.

Environments That Promote Multilingualism

The final visible expression of a shared vision is found in the environment itself. Schools that value MLs make that value unmistakable. As described in more detail in Chapter 2 in the section "Representation," hallway displays, library collections, morning announcements, school events, and classroom routines reflect the linguistic and cultural diversity of the rural community. Bilingual signage signals welcome and belonging; however, bilingual materials are too frequently absent from the school, beginning with a welcome sign at the main door and instructions for ML families on how to access the front office. A bilingual sign demonstrating a welcoming environment is in Figure 3.5. Multilingual celebrations mark essential cultural traditions and invite families into the school space as honored participants. Classroom libraries feature texts that represent students' languages and identities, and digital tools enable students to access content in multiple languages.

These environmental markers communicate a powerful message: multilingualism is not a barrier to overcome but a resource to cultivate (Ruiz, 1984). When students see their languages affirmed publicly, their engagement and sense of belonging increase. Rural teachers, too, benefit from an environment that constantly reinforces the shared vision. The environment becomes a daily reminder of the community's commitments and a catalyst for encouraging staff to expand their instructional practices. In rural communities, where multilingualism may previously have been invisible, these efforts carry particular weight. They disrupt stereotypes and broaden understandings of who belongs in the community. They create bridges between long-time residents and newcomer families. Most importantly, they provide MLs with visibility and voice.

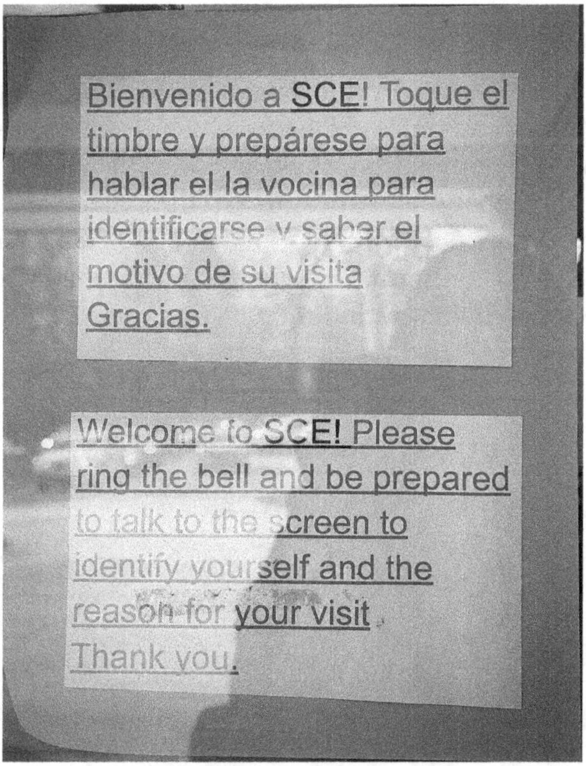

FIGURE 3.5 Bilingual school welcome sign. Image by the author.

Together, these practices move a shared vision from aspiration to action. They demonstrate that rural schools, even with limited resources, can cultivate coherent, inclusive, and linguistically affirming environments for MLs. By anchoring daily routines, instructional decisions, and collaborative structures in a shared sense of purpose, educators create a system in which MLs thrive and rural schools become vibrant centers of equity and opportunity.

Conclusion

This chapter described rural educators establishing a shared vision for their ML students and families. A shared vision in rural ML education is not only a pedagogical framework but also a rural community imperative and cultural commitment.

This chapter echoes Jeanette Thurber's conviction that a truly democratic educational system must reflect and serve all members of its community. In the same way that her vision helped shape the American musical legacy, which resulted in a uniquely American symphony with influences from Black spiritual music and Indigenous sounds, educators' shared vision today shapes what rural schools can become: inclusive, collaborative, asset-driven learning communities where multilingualism and cultural diversity are their foundational strengths.

DISCUSSION QUESTIONS FOR CHAPTER 3

1. If you were to write a vision for MLs in your school, what would it be? What would you like for them to experience, engage in, and achieve? Are these achievements academic or social, or both?
2. What short-, medium-, and long-term goals would a shared vision for rural MLs look like in your rural school?
3. Who would you include in an ML team that creates a shared vision for MLs in your school? Think beyond teachers to include staff who are engaged with MLs and their families, bilingual liaison staff, and school staff. How could you convene this group and build vision, community, and cohesion to support MLs and their families?

4

The Third Movement

Centering Multilingual Learner Families

Look there at the little village with the long name of Nelahozeves and there just below the castle of the Prince Lobkowicz, that low building, do you see it? That's where my father had his inn, at the same time carried on his trade of a butcher. It was in that little house that I was born and here in this lovely countryside that I spent my poor childhood. The little church there, that's where I played my first violin solo and what a fuss I was in that time and how afraid I was when I tuned my fiddle and how my bow shook at the first notes. But it turned out all right. When I had finished, there was a hum and a buzz throughout the whole choir. Everybody pressed round me, my friends smiled happily at me and clapped me on the back good-naturedly. And our neighbor, the leader of the violins, gave me a whole groschen. That was a happier side of my youth, the brighter moments. But even the darker side was not uninteresting though it cost me many a tear. Look there, these are the places I used to visit with my father to buy all kinds of cattle beasts. And when my father entrusted me with one or other member of the brute creation, it would often out of sheer exuberance, give me the slip or without more ado, dragged me into the nearest pond so that my

DOI: 10.4324/9781003509875-4

> situation was not exactly enviable, but all the calamities and trials of my young life were sweetened by music, my guardian angel.
>
> —*Memories of Antonín Dvořák*

Introduction

Dvořák's roseate memory of his rural childhood—rich with music, family, labor, and community—reflects the essence of what rural multilingual families bring to their communities and the knowledge that they impart. His recollection highlights a central truth: that even in economically modest and physically demanding environments, joy, creativity, and deep learning flourish. The local church where he played violin, the family-run inn, the muddy cattle trips with his father—these were not barriers to learning, but the context in which his artistry and resilience were shaped. Yet such narratives, shaped by retrospection and selective remembrance, also risk obscuring the uneven conditions under which rural families live and learn, particularly those whose languages, labor, and identities are marginalized. For educators, this underscores a powerful message: rural families, often viewed through deficit lenses, possess cultural wealth and experiential knowledge that are fundamental to their children's development. Like Dvořák's early musical experiences, ML family engagement must begin with recognition of these lived experiences and build from them with honor, trust, and authentic collaboration.

Part I: What It Is

The third principle of creating equity spaces of hope for rural ML students and families involves the process of recentering ML families in family engagement practices across the spectrum of educational programs, policies, and practices. What is "recentering" in family engagement? And why is recentering important?

Families are central to child development and learning, but ML families' strengths and knowledge are often absent from the engagement practices enacted in schools. Rural educators who work with ML students and families have lamented over the past 30 years that one of their biggest challenges is engaging ML families in their child's education (Coady et al., 2015). Exit data from our preservice teacher education programs repeatedly reveal that, unless our teacher candidates have completed targeted coursework in ML family engagement, graduates report feeling *least prepared* to work with non-English-speaking families (Coady et al., 2011).

Similarly, practicing educators often state that they simply cannot identify how to get ML families to "show up" in school, to participate in ESL information sessions or parent-teacher meetings, or to attend school events that would assist their child, such as completing the FAFSA (Free Application for Federal Student Aid) for college applications. In addition, schools that receive funding under Title I (Every Student Succeeds Act, 2015, § 1116), for serving low-wealth families, and Title III (Every Student Succeeds Act, 2015, § 3115), for families with students identified as MLs, must ensure participation of those families in their educational programs and report back on these data (U.S. Department of Education, 2016). Thus, ML family engagement is not only a matter of good practice and support for child development and learning, but it is also a requirement for many schools. The need for ML family engagement remains a priority among educators, given the effects of families on children's learning and development.

As described in Chapter 1, rural schools do not operate in the same ways as their suburban or urban counterparts, due in part to the disproportionate access to and availability of resources, particularly as the number of ML students increases. Distance to schools and access to transportation, for instance, affect the likelihood that many ML families can attend school events. Rural families who work in seasonal industries, such as crop labor, have variable work schedules. Poultry workers, such as turkey catchers, work at sundown and into the evenings when animals are less active. Many families maintain two or three jobs to make ends meet and travel long distances to work.

These contextual factors in rural schools affect families' ability to attend the events that schools traditionally consider indicators of family engagement. Rural language professionals (ESL teachers, bilingual teachers, paraeducators) describe the persistent challenges they face, despite using all of the usual strategies of family engagement: sending notes home to families in their home language, organizing evening meetings outside of working hours, offering babysitting or childcare, and providing an evening meal or snacks. Given these supports and suggestions, why does ML family engagement remain problematic for rural educators?

Recentering ML families in school practices is a key principle of improving learning and well-being for rural ML students. In this chapter, I argue that while rural ML family engagement and involvement are essential to student learning, the basic premise on which the concept of "family engagement" for ML families is predicated fundamentally contradicts a strengths-based, linguistically and culturally responsive approach to family engagement. Traditional Western concepts of family, school, education, and engagement are misaligned with the strengths, knowledge, experiences, and ways of knowing and being of linguistically and culturally diverse families. Here, I propose new ideas and a reconceptualization of ML family engagement, shifting from school-based, compliance-driven to family-centered, family-driven.

Family Engagement and Family Involvement: What's the Difference?

In this book, particularly regarding families as a fundamental principle of ML education, I use the term "family engagement." I refer to family engagement as an ongoing process centered on relationships of trust and care between educators, ML families, and students. Scholars have defined family *engagement* as various activities in which families participate that can lead to positive learning outcomes for children. For instance, the National Association for Family, School, and Community Engagement (NAFSCE, 2024) defines family engagement as having three key components: (1) a shared responsibility where schools and other agencies reach out to families in meaningful ways and are committed to child learning and development, (2) a continuous and enduring commitment across a child's life, and (3) a reinforcement of learning that takes place across multiple settings (school, home, community). NAFSCE continues that "high impact" family engagement is collaborative, culturally responsive, and based on relationships of respect and understanding. Building upon that definition, ML family engagement includes those elements but further adds language and communication, as well as a recentering of engagement around the ontologies (that is, the identities) and epistemologies (that is, the knowledges) of the families themselves.

In contrast, family *involvement*, which is more prevalent across the education literature, refers to the responsibilities of families to "get involved" in their child's education. In other words, the actions and work are incumbent upon families. In their work with Latino adolescents, Ceballo et al. (2014) define parental involvement as the resources parents dedicate to their children's education. The concept of involvement assumes that parents or families are responsible for initiating actions and interactions with schools. This is a narrower view of the actual activities, supports, and experiences of families in the context of their child's learning and education. Even the notion of involvement can be culturally biased. For instance, in some non-Western cultures, parents and extended family members' role in children's learning is to ensure that their children are respectful toward teachers and behave appropriately in school. This contrasts with Western ideas of family involvement, in which educators typically expect parents to participate in traditional school events, such as the PTA (Parent-Teacher Association), attend school field trips with their children, and volunteer time and resources at the school.

The relationship between engagement and involvement has been examined along a continuum (Goodall & Montgomery, 2014), with one end representing *parental involvement with schools* and the other representing *parental engagement with learning*. Parental involvement with schools generally entails school-led actions. In contrast, at the other end of the continuum, engagement is parent-led and parent-devised. Goodall and Montgomery suggest that the middle ground lies in *parental involvement in schooling,* in which parents and educators collaborate to plan activities. According to the authors, the difference across these points on the continuum lies in who (parents or school) has agency over the activities, events, and direction of the child's learning. Strong parental engagement exists when there is a "shift in relation to action and responsibility," in which parents or caregivers determine what engagement entails and how it unfolds (p. 406). For educators working with ML families, the concept of family engagement requires reconsideration from nontraditional perspectives.

Why Families Matter in Education

Decades of research point to the benefits of family engagement for children's learning and education. Scholars have written extensively and synthesized research on family involvement. They conclude across the research studies that there is a strong, positive association between family involvement and student achievement (Epstein, 2011; Henderson & Mapp, 2002; Jeynes, 2003), yet at the same time, there is no one-size-fits-all approach to family participation in child education precisely because communities function differently, have different resource bases, and need to be responsive to differing and changing family demographics (Téllez & Waxman, 2010).

Scholars note that recognizing family strengths and the roles of class difference, cultural background, and family needs in learning are key to effective family engagement. Some scholars have synthesized research on diverse families, including ML families (e.g., Jeynes, 2003). That work found that when parents convey high expectations to their children, it has a positive impact on their learning. Broadly speaking, research on family engagement consistently highlights several common practices that support ML students and families: *communication* between families and educators (Deslandes et al., 1997) that respond to the cultural and linguistic repertoires of families; varied types of *participation* in and outside of school, ranging from traditional school events such as parent-teacher conferences and PTAs to family culture fairs and home literacy events (Goodall & Montgomery, 2014; Protacio et al., 2020); and *assistance* for children that supports home learning and strengthens family relationships and child well-being (Shumow & Miller, 2001).

Several studies that synthesize research findings, known as meta-analyses, underscore these findings. For instance, in large-scale studies that include linguistically and culturally diverse students and families, two main areas appeared to affect student learning significantly: parental (caregiver) *communication* with the child, including conversations related to school experiences, home learning, and the importance of education, and conveying high *expectations* of the child, such as completing schoolwork and their future education plans—for instance, attending college (Jeynes, 2003). This work shows that parental involvement has a significant positive effect on children across racial, ethnic, social class, and linguistic groups.

In another meta-analysis of U.S. K–12 public schools, scholars found a strong positive association between family involvement and student achievement (Henderson & Mapp, 2002). The most effective activities appeared to build upon families' strengths, recognize class and cultural differences, and address specific family needs. In a more recent meta-analysis, scholars found that the strongest associations between family engagement and ML student learning were observed when families held high expectations for their child's learning and high aspirations for further learning (He & Thompson, 2022). These data underscore the earlier findings from research syntheses reported by Jeynes (2003, 2017).

As educators, the policies and practices we initiate regarding how and when to engage families have been based on handed-down beliefs and ideas about what families should do. These beliefs have been explored by scholars working with ML students and families. Baquedano-López et al. (2014) describe three "tropes" of ML family engagement. Tropes are clichés or stereotypes, and in this case, they serve to minimize or oversimplify the complexity of families and their roles in education. Baquedano-López and colleagues identified these three tropes:

- Parents as first teachers
- Parents as learners
- Parents as partners

Tropes serve to mask inequities in education and to diminish the power of parents. In the case of ML families, certain aspects of family functioning may differ from educators' beliefs about family engagement. The three tropes underscore an unconscious view that parents must behave in a certain way (such as enacting work that is taken up by the school teacher) or be remedied in ways the school requires.

The *parents-as-first-teachers* trope acknowledges that all parents are their children's first teachers, yet this trope deems low-income parents and parents of color as incapable of fulfilling this role. This trope implies that low-income parents of color are inherently incapable of successfully fulfilling this role, requiring funded programs to transfer educational responsibilities. Assumptions about nondominant families often drive the *parents-as-learners trope*. It aims to teach parents how to navigate the school system explicitly. This trope promotes changing the diverse family to accommodate the school's agenda, and regards minoritized parents as "uneducated" and in need of instruction. Finally, the *parents-as-partners* trope relies on a conception of family partnerships that can be misleading, as it promotes a specific type of relationship. It uses middle-class parents as the norm or exemplar, while implicitly targeting parents of color as needing to be "engaged" and "involved" as partners (Baquedano-López et al., 2014). The aforementioned tropes assume that ML families function like English-speaking families, who generally share the same cultural backgrounds as the school and community.

Shim (2013) examined rural ML family engagement and identified several obstacles that hindered the development of parent-teacher relationships. Generally, ML families reported that educators judged them, were frustrated by their limited influence on teachers' decision-making, and were afraid to speak up due to potential repercussions. Ultimately, Shim determined that structural factors and power asymmetries too often characterize the relationships between teachers and families.

I argue that ML family engagement employs a different lens for understanding and enacting the relationship between schools and homes, or between educators and families. Scholars have noted that nontraditional activities with ML families provide greater support to students and are more likely to foster strong relationships and support for learning. For instance, Arias and Morillo-Campbell (2008) describe the need for families and educators to collaborate in building a reciprocal understanding of schools and expectations for student learning. They also found that educators could foster and support parent-initiated engagement efforts. Because ML families represent a diverse range of languages and cultural backgrounds, educators are responsible for ensuring that school practices with families are both linguistically and culturally appropriate.

Shifting Concepts

As we shift ideas and concepts about ML family engagement, it becomes evident that families lie at the heart of engagement practices. Earlier in this book, we examined rural cultural wealth and key concepts related to rural strengths. These are summarized in Table 4.1.

Many ML families demonstrate these strengths in their everyday lives. For instance, in an early Head Start program serving Latino families, *familismo*—a concept encompassing commitment, dedication, and loyalty to family—was essential to family participation and engagement in the program (Morales-Alexander, 2021).

TABLE 4.1 Rural Cultural Wealth from Crumb et al. (2022)

Rural Cultural Wealth Theory
Rural resourcefulness (the capacity of rural people to meet and overcome social and contextual adversities)
Rural ingenuity (a characteristic of the collective community as people leverage everyday knowledge to respond creatively to challenges and by using local resources)
Rural familism (intergenerational relationships, family geographic proximity, and family lineage reinforce collective care and social networks)
Rural community unity (how community members organize and unify for civic engagement and collaboration, particularly in times of need)

When extended family members were involved, and the group adopted collectivist caring practices, families became more engaged in their children's education.

Other concepts about family engagement have been derived from studies with Latino families. Their backgrounds have surfaced in the research as positive factors that support ML students, including *respeto* (respect), *convivencia* (coexistence), *confianza* (trust), and *comunicación* (communication). For instance, in their work, Flores et al. (2019) examined outcomes associated with strong family engagement among Latino families at Gene Ward Elementary School in Nevada. Over five years, they identified spaces dedicated to Latino families that included childcare and extended family members. They also found that educators involved in school governance and administration had to relinquish authority over family engagement in favor of a "by families for families" approach. Other scholars have argued that teachers need to reconceptualize engagement and literacy and to recognize the multiple, diverse literacy practices that ML families regularly engage in (Coady, 2009; Morita-Mullaney, 2021). For instance, I found that rural ML families' home literacy practices included print from biblical sources translated into an Indigenous language, oral literacy practices surrounding culinary and cooking among women, and religious iconography, maps, and calendars that adorned the household. Not only did these reflect literacy activities, but they also revealed the rich cultural background and histories of rural ML families in the community.

ML families rely on and build upon their ways of knowing and being to participate in the world around them. The strengths they bring include their histories, traditional and cultural knowledge, skills, and habits; language and literacy practices; social network and survival skills (Moll et al., 1992); and contributions to community functioning. Schissel (2025) argues for a humanizing lens that centers ML communities and their experiences and histories. Educators need to understand the existing histories and prior experiences of ML families with education.

Overall, we can draw meaningful conclusions about ML family engagement from decades of research. First, ML family engagement with diverse immigrant and language-minoritized families' needs to shift away from traditional approaches, such as physical presence in the classroom or participation in the PTA, and toward recognizing and affirming the linguistically and culturally relevant activities that families already engage in with their children. Second, although there is no one-size-fits-all approach, given the diversity of communities and families, the most effective engagement practices center on who families are, families' needs, affirming home languages and cultures, and reframing "engagement" from the family's perspective rather than from the school's. There are models of family engagement that incorporate these key ideas. Next, I describe what recentering families in family engagement entails and introduce new concepts, such as *consejos, tequio,* and transcolonizing, to reimagine this work.

Consejos, Tequio, and Transcolonizing

Building on rural and cultural strengths, we can turn to three concepts that illustrate how multilingual families live engagement in their daily lives: *consejos, tequio,* and *transcolonizing*. Each of these concepts offers a lens for reimagining family engagement from the inside out, shifting from familial practices within the home to collective community action, and ultimately to systemic transformation. By 'systemic transformation' I am referring to changes that are made to larger systems such as schools, districts, and states that embed these practices. These ideas build on one another, each with its own rhythm, tone, and texture, yet together they create a fuller harmony of how families teach, organize, and transform within rural communities. Read in sequence, *consejos, tequio,* and transcolonizing form a progression: from the soft harmonies of home teachings, to the steady drumbeat of community engagement, to the crescendo of structural change.

Consejos

Consejos are everyday forms of oral teaching that circulate within multilingual families. They often take the form of brief conversations, sayings, warnings, and personal stories through which parents—most often mothers—guide their children's moral and educational choices. Delgado-Gaitán (1994) describes consejos as a form of "nurturing advice," conveyed through family conversations that transmit values, experiences, and guidance to children as they navigate schooling and everyday life (p. 298).

Research on first-generation Latina college students similarly shows how these family messages shape educational persistence. Martínez-Cortés and Romo (2025) explain that "consejos about education, resiliency, and persistence were integral to the students' ability to remain motivated and continue pursuing their college goals" (p. 12). As one participant in their study recalled, "My parents always told me that education was the one thing nobody could take away from me" (Martínez-Cortés & Romo, 2025, p. 11). Within these intimate exchanges, families articulate both aspiration and resistance, transforming migration and labor experiences into lessons of perseverance and hope while framing education as a pathway toward improved futures.

In this sense, consejos are a micro-level expression of familial and aspirational capital (Yosso, 2005). They occur within the home and among extended kin, sustaining emotional bonds and reinforcing collective values about effort, humility, and mutual care. For educators, recognizing consejos means understanding that family engagement begins long before parents enter a school building. Teachers can honor this pedagogy of care by inviting families to share consejos through bilingual story circles, classroom newsletters, or audio recordings that connect lived wisdom to students' learning. Listening to consejos repositions families as educators whose words continue to shape their children's sense of purpose and belonging.

Tequio

The second concept is *tequio*. At the community, or meso, level, tequio represents the extension of family-based values of care and cooperation into public life. Defined as unpaid communal labor carried out for the collective good, tequio is rooted in Indigenous systems of reciprocity that emphasize interdependence and shared responsibility among community members. Rather than viewing labor as individual volunteerism, tequio reflects a collective obligation to sustain the well-being of the community. De la Fuente (1989, as cited in Jasis & Ordoñez-Jasis, 2012) describes tequio as communal work carried out "[to] improv[e] the life and the future of the community and of future generations" (p. 80) often accompanied by celebration, social renewal, and the reaffirmation of community ties.

Research on Latino immigrant families demonstrates that these values frequently guide how multilingual families engage with schools and communities. Jasis and Ordoñez-Jasis (2012) found that immigrant parents often draw on traditions of collective cooperation when organizing for equitable schooling. In their study, Latina mothers mobilized networks of support that transformed parent participation from individual volunteering into collective advocacy and school improvement. For example, families coordinated community workdays to clean and repair school facilities, beautify shared spaces, and create environments that reflected the culture and language of their children. These efforts reflected a commitment not only to the school itself but to the well-being and dignity of the broader community.

Practices such as *tequio* reflect broader Indigenous practices of reciprocity found across Latin America. In the Andean regions of Peru, Bolivia, and Ecuador, Quechua and Aymara communities organize social life through the principle of *ayni*, an ethic of mutual aid often translated as 'today for you, tomorrow for me.' Through ayni, families contribute labor to assist others in tasks such as building homes, planting or harvesting crops, or organizing community events, with the understanding that such support will be reciprocated when needed (Allen, 1988; Mannheim, 1986; Walsh-Dilley, 2017). Rather than functioning as charity or volunteerism, ayni operates as a relational system that sustains community life and reinforces shared responsibility among community members.

These traditions illuminate how communal responsibility operates not as charity but as a relational system that sustains social and communal life. While conducting work at a rural, under resourced school in Alabama, immigrant families spent one weekend each year in the spring to collectively gather and beautify the school in keeping with their view of the collective contribution and care. This became embedded into the school culture. Within rural communities, such systems align closely with Crumb et al.'s (2022) concept of rural community unity—the capacity of community members to organize collaboratively, particularly in times of need. When multilingual families bring these traditions of cooperation into school spaces, they are drawing upon deeply rooted cultural knowledge about how communities function and thrive.

Educators can build upon these traditions by designing engagement opportunities that reflect collective participation rather than individual volunteerism. Schools can partner with families to organize community workdays, establish bilingual school gardens, or co-create cultural events that celebrate the languages and histories of the community. When families collaborate in these efforts, engagement becomes a shared responsibility grounded in reciprocity and collective care. In this way, *tequio* provides a powerful lens for understanding how multilingual families extend familial values into broader community action, transforming schools into spaces where collaboration, dignity, and shared responsibility guide educational partnerships.

Transcolonizing

Building on the interpersonal and communal dimensions of *consejos* and *tequio*, transcolonizing calls for systemic transformation and a rethinking of how schools relate to multilingual families and whose knowledge guides educational life. Schissel (2025) defines a humanizing educational lens as one that operates through "three overlapping areas: decolonizing, historicizing, and communing actions" (p. 2). Decolonizing recovers "ways of seeing, talking about, and interacting with the world that have been violently uprooted… and supplanted by those of the institutions of predominant power" (p. 2). Historicizing asks educators to "understand the cumulative impact and legacies of harm experienced by minoritized communities," while communing centers "minoritized communities' purposes and experiences" (p. 5).

At this macro level, transcolonizing reframes family engagement beyond school-centric, compliance-based models of parent involvement as a shared practice that guides how schools work with families rather than as an occasional activity or event.

Women, especially multilingual mothers who sustain kinship and community networks, often lead this transformation. Their organizing mirrors the communing Schissel describes and reflects the women-led activism documented by Jasis and Ordoñez-Jasis (2012): collective leadership grounded in reciprocity and care. For instance, transcolonizing engagement might appear when educators and families design participatory mapping projects that document local labor histories and linguistic contributions. When schools invite these leaders to co-create curriculum, family councils, or participatory research, they enact what Schissel (2025) calls "a change in priorities from goals and standards of a profession to lived realities of people" (p. 20). Transcolonizing thus becomes a new ethic of collaboration, one in which multilingual women's voices reshape not only educational practices but also the culture of schooling itself.

Played in concert, *consejos*, *tequio*, and transcolonizing reveal a continuum of family engagement that moves from the personal to the collective to the systemic. Each concept carries its own rhythm yet contributes to a larger harmony of care, reciprocity, and transformation. They remind educators that change begins in the everyday acts of guidance within homes, expands through collaborative community work, and culminates in reimagining the very structures of schooling. Engagement, in this sense, becomes both practice and purpose, a shared song of belonging, dignity, and hope for families and communities.

The next section, "What It Looks Like," turns from concept to practice, showing how the ideas explored in this Third Movement take shape in families, schools, and communities. Here, educators and families translate the harmonies of *consejos*, *tequio*, and transcolonizing into daily acts of teaching, learning, and care. Their work demonstrates that family-centered engagement is not a program to be implemented but a relationship to be lived: an improvisation responsive to local rhythms, resources, and needs. In moving from theory to application, this section illustrates how the principles of reciprocity, collaboration, and cultural sustainability become tangible in rural multilingual classrooms and partnerships.

Part II: What It Looks Like

When I attend ML family engagement events, one of the first things I frequently notice is just how silent families often are. ML families may be U.S.-based or may have immigrated from other countries. Their stories are powerful, varied, unique, sometimes painful, and frequently hopeful. They have significant experience that has brought them to that exact position in your school. But how much do you know about their stories? And how much do they know about each other's stories?

Unless people talk, interact, and share, they cannot build relationships that lead to networks of support and care. Just as we know that all students in school need to speak and interact through collaboration, learning, and sharing, the same is true for ML families. Silence among families during family engagement events, or when families are recipients of information rather than primary sources or co-creators of information, indicates that more or different types of communication are needed among ML families.

As described in Chapter 2, Ms. Quintero's work as a principal and former migrant worker in Florida has been highly successful in her family engagement events. During the COVID-19 pandemic, Ms. Quintero reported that approximately 95 families attended weekly Zoom meetings. She had built relationships with families over many years, and she and her family were members of the rural community. She began her work at the school as a staff member in family engagement, which gave her time and professional expertise to get to know her families. She understood the context in which they came to the United States, specifically the crop industry, primarily focused on oranges, that they worked in, as well as the migratory journeys of many families north each year in pursuit of seasonal crops. For Ms. Quintero, knowing the families was central to her success. For her, family engagement was more than a check on a checklist or, as noted earlier, a compliance task. She built relationships with the families, listened intently to their concerns, identified solutions, and consistently followed up with them. Families, in return, trusted Zulaika and the school staff.

At one of our partner rural schools, I observed that families were indeed overwhelmingly silent during the engagement events. At one of the ESL family nights at the beginning of the school year, educators meticulously prepared materials and planned activities to welcome new ML families and to introduce them to the ESL program. The evening was intended to provide families with the required information on the ESL program, the WIDA (wida.us) system for English language development, and the WIDA ACCESS 2.0 English language proficiency test, administered each February, and results provided to families early in the school year. Educators also aimed to encourage home reading between parent and child, so they planned an activity in which parents participated in a read-aloud with their child using the book *Too Many Tamales* (Soto, 1993). Following the read-aloud, the ESL staff provided parents with questions to ask their child about the story's plot, characters, and main idea. The educators ended the evening event with pizza and juice.

As I watched this scene unfold, it reminded me of numerous one-way family events in which parents were the recipients of information and educators were the depositors. This resonated with Freire's (1970) "banking" concept of education, which contrasts with humanizing pedagogy that centers on relationships, sharing, and community knowledge. In banking education, educators who hold knowledge deposit information into their students' minds, just as people would deposit money into a bank account. In contrast, humanizing pedagogy reframes education to be grounded in relationships that see, honor, and affirm people. It is based on the idea that all people know "things," and whose knowledge is prioritized and valued, reflects minoritized peoples' experiences and identities. Learning occurs through relationships that illuminate previously invisible knowledge as people together co-construct it through discourse.

One of the Latina teachers at the school, Marta, and her husband, Miguel, noted that the ML families were from diverse cultural and geographic backgrounds, Mexican, Guatemalan, Honduran, Salvadoran, Chilean, and Panamanian. Despite sharing a common language, they had no regular communication with one another. This distressed Miguel tremendously because, he stated, without relational networks and collaboration, the families could not organize to voice their needs, ask questions about school programs and their child's learning, participate in school events, or receive information on much-needed services in their rural community.

As a result of this conversation, Marta and I planned to change the ESL nights to refocus them on the families' backgrounds and knowledge. We began by talking with several families individually and asking what they knew about the school programs and what they wanted to know. We also asked what needs they had that would help them navigate their child's school and educational program. One school had a rural DLI (rDLI) program, which therefore had bilingual teachers, and other schools had ESL teachers and bilingual family liaison staff who traveled between schools. Marta and I created a "*Quién es quien en la escuela de mi hijo/a?*—Who is Who in My Child's School?" handout (Figure 4.1), which provided definitions and descriptions of school staff roles. We had families place a star and add the contact information, such as telephone number for WhatsApp or text messages, for staff that could communicate in Spanish. At the next ESL family night, we arranged the room into small-group tables and allocated time for families to meet and greet one another. We modeled how to use the handout and had families identify the person they needed to contact, for instance, if their child was sick or they experienced a bullying incident.

Families began to discuss and share information about the community's bilingual resources and how to use them. For instance, a local community college offered adult ESL classes during the day. For some families, having young children at home was a barrier to attending ESL. Families established a network through which some cared for the children while others attended ESL classes.

In addition to resource building and sharing, Marta and I reorganized the next ESL night to create space for families to indicate where they were from and to show it on a map. At that ESL family engagement event, ML families entered the school cafeteria and signed in. Subsequently, they were invited to use a sticky paper arrow and place it on the map near the region or

Quién es quién en la escuela de mi hijo/a
Who is Who in My Child's School

Maestro(a) de inglés como segundo idioma– la persona encargada del aprendizaje de mi hijo(a)
English as a Second Language (ESL) Teacher – the person in charge of my child's learning
Nombre/Name______________________________

Director(a) – la persona encargada de la escuela, el/la líder
Director or Principal – the person in charge of the school, the school leader
Nombre/Name____________________________

Director(a) Asistente Subdirector(a)* – la persona encargada—en general—del comportamiento de los alumnos
Assistant Director or Vice Principal – the person sometimes in charge of student behavior in school. Nombre/Name______________________________

Secretaria de la escuela / School secretary
Nombre/Name______________________________

Asistente bilingüe – una persona bilingüe que ayuda a el/la maestro(a)
Bilingual aide – a bilingual person or classroom aide who helps the teacher
Nombre/Name______________________________

Trabajador(a) social– una persona encargada de ayudar a mi hijo(a) en sus relaciones familiares y sociales, en sus amistades, así como en su horario escolar y orientación vocacional.
Guidance Counselor – the person in charge of helping my child with family, social, friend relationships, with her school schedule, and materials for further education.
Nombre/Name______________________________

Maestro(a) – la persona encargada del aprendizaje de mi hijo(a)
Teacher – the person in charge of my child's learning
Nombre/Name______________________________

FIGURE 4.1 Quién es quien en la escuela de mi hijo/a?—Who is in my child's school? handout by the author.

FIGURE 4.2 Rural ML families at a family engagement event. Image by the author.

country from which they were. What resulted from this small change was remarkable. Parents told and showed their children where they were from, and how they arrived in the U.S. These were stories the children had not known. The families could also see where other families were from and learned about the diverse languages and cultures in their own rural community. Figure 4.2 depicts an ML family at a rural school family engagement event, where parents showed their children their home countries. Figure 4.3 shows a map of the countries of origin of the children's families.

In this district, families became closer over two years. They came to learn how the school system operated and how to establish parallel organizations to share information and participate equally in their children's education. For example, while working

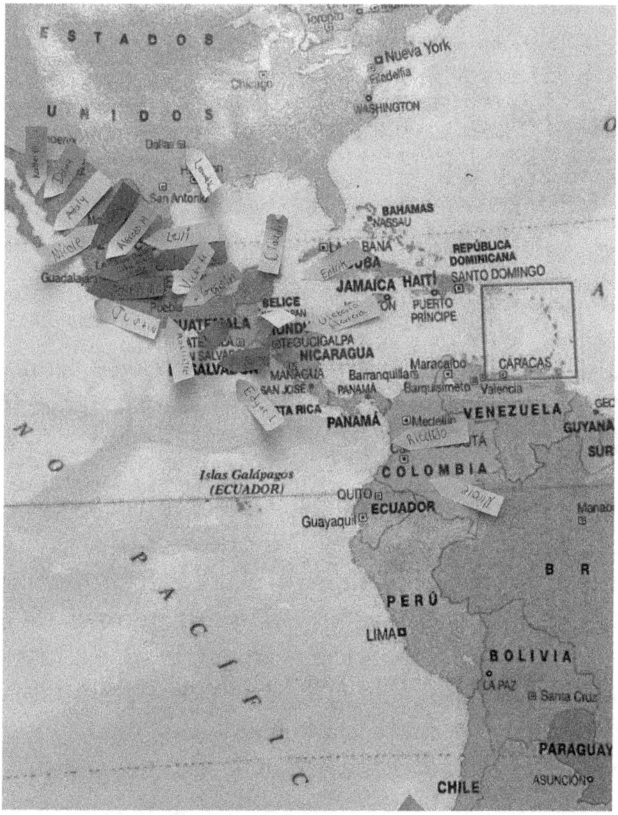

FIGURE 4.3 Map of the home countries of rural ML families. Image by the author.

with a bilingual principal of a rural dual language immersion (rDLI) program, Spanish-speaking families requested their own PTA. The Spanish PTA was open to all families, but it operated primarily in Spanish, with interpretation available for non-Spanish speakers. This was a bold step for ML families in a rural school district but demonstrates the dedication and commitment to their child's education, agency, and community-building.

Over time, I have developed additional resources that can be used and adapted for ML families to learn how the school district functions and to build communication strategies. I have found that apps and electronic resources can be helpful, but can be more intimidating to families than traditional print materials. In addition to the fotonovelas described in Chapter 2, translation of phrases

español	inglés
Hola.	Hello.
No sé hablar inglés.	I don't know how to speak English.
¿Puedo hablar con alguien en español?	May I speak with someone who speaks Spanish?
¿Puedo hacer una cita para hablar con alguien en español?	Can I make an appointment with someone in Spanish?
El nombre de mi hijo/a es___________.	My child's name is____________.
Mi hijo/a tiene __________ años.	My child I __________ years old.
Mi número de teléfono es ______________________.	My telephone number is __________________.
Necesito inscriber a mi hijo/a en la escuela.	I need to enroll my child in school.
Mi hijo/a está enfermo/a hoy.	Mi child is sick today.
¿Puedo hablar con la maestra de mi hijo/a?	Can I speak with my child's teacher?

FIGURE 4.4 Point-to phrases and translation. Handout by the author.

that families can point to at the school office or while in meetings can reduce the stress of producing oral language in English (Figure 4.4).

Rural Cultural Wealth in Multilingual Communities

Finally, as we return to the recentering of ML families in rural communities, it is evident that rural resourcefulness, familism, and unity are concepts that are rooted in human relationships that move away from individual concepts of success to collective patterns of engagement (Table 4.2). Multilingual families in rural settings demonstrate remarkable resourcefulness as they navigate educational systems. When educators reframe ML family engagement based on the identities and knowledge of ML families, ML families actively build networks to support their children's learning and *educación*.

TABLE 4.2 Crumb et al. (2022) with Examples from Coady

Theory	*Examples from ML Communities*
Rural Cultural Wealth (Crumb et al., 2022)	
Rural resourcefulness (the capacity of rural people to meet and overcome social and contextual adversities)	ML families network to understand how schools work and seek more explicit support. Families identify educators who speak their languages. They reach out to family engagement specialists or other educators for "other" non-school-related needs, but that are essential to their well-being. For instance, they may ask for translation for school and non-school-related documents, or how to navigate policies. Transcolonizing aligns to rural resourcefulness and the ability to overcome adversity and identify solutions outside of traditional systems.

(*continued*)

TABLE 4.2 (continued)

Theory	*Examples from ML Communities*
Rural ingenuity (a characteristic of the collective community as people leverage everyday knowledge to respond creatively to challenges and by using local resources)	A bilingual ESL teacher works through her networks as a Spanish speaker to identify how ML families can be better served through language services at information sessions, such as a high school FAFSA event, or assisting a child to apply to college. Family engagement specialists or school counselors' roles are flexible, and they find resources for families through online translation, local community organizers or nonprofit organizations, and educators in the district who can assist.
Rural familism (intergenerational relationships, family geographic proximity, and family lineage reinforce collective care and social networks)	Intergenerational family members are invited to participate in family engagement events. Including extended family members helps ML families to build networks of support. ML families may rely on neighbors to drive children to school if they are working. Families establish collective care structures and build a language and cultural social network. *Tequio* and collective dedication align with extended family in *familismo*.
Rural community unity (how community members organize and unify for civic engagement and collaboration, particularly in times of need)	Rural educators build school- and classroom- level community unity to support each other in their work; the rural bilingual liaisons and family engagement specialists use insider knowledge and relationships to assist families. They build trust through shared language and culture, *tequio*, and collective dedication to the rural community.
Place-Conscious Education (Greenwood, 2019) is an ongoing process of reflection, unlearning, and reinhabitation, and involves interrogating learned colonial practices and mindsets	Educators identify the stories and histories of all people (ML, Indigenous, minoritized) who inhabit the rural community, and how ML families contribute to community functioning. Educators would ask why ML families might not be represented in social systems and structures, why they may be quiet at meetings or events, and how schools can disrupt the silence. Educators need to unlearn traditional family engagement practices and reflect on and recenter families using their languages and cultures as starting points.

Rural resourcefulness is complemented by families' funds of knowledge (Moll et al., 1992) found within their community. When rural schools leverage their language skills and professional networks through bilingual staff and paraeducators, teachers, and leaders, they can reframe ML family engagement to center the strengths of families. ML families demonstrate resourcefulness and transcolonizing practices through their ability to overcome adversity and identify nontraditional solutions. The strength of intergenerational relationships—what researchers call rural familism—further enriches these communities. Extended family members participate in school events, building broader networks of support. Neighbors step in to drive children to school when parents are working. Through these everyday acts of care, families create collective structures that sustain both language and culture across generations. Rural community unity manifests in how educators themselves come together. Bilingual liaisons and family engagement specialists draw on insider knowledge and trusted relationships to assist families, building bridges through shared language and cultural understanding.

Finally, a place-conscious approach to rural ML family engagement calls upon educators to reflect deeply on whose stories are told and who remains invisible within rural communities. This means asking why multilingual families may be quiet at meetings, how schools might be perpetuating silence, and what it would look like to unlearn traditional practices and recenter families' languages and cultures as the foundation for meaningful engagement.

Conclusion

This chapter examines rural ML family engagement practices and challenges traditional frameworks and practices that continue to position ML families from a deficit perspective. I argue that there are new and exciting ways to engage ML families where their knowledge (cultural, linguistic) and identities are centered in our work. Educators' work is to serve as a bridge between rural school practices and their functioning, and the expertise that diverse ML families bring to the school and community. Too often, these are hidden and out of view of educators and staff. Concepts of *consejos*, *tequio*, and transcolonizing offer new ways to frame and enact family engagement practices. Moreover, local, place-based histories can inform educators' work and reimagine family engagement that reflects shared rural community spaces.

DISCUSSION QUESTIONS FOR CHAPTER 4

1 This chapter discussed three "tropes" surrounding ML families. What tropes can you identify in the messaging in your school? In your district? How can you challenge these tropes?

2 What industries do ML families in your rural community work in? How does the school district, school, and classroom engage with their knowledge? How can you bring their expertise, including language expertise, into your school in ways and at times that are convenient for them?

3 Convene a group of ML families with cultural sensitivity and language interpretation supports. What barriers do they report to engaging with the school? What kinds of networks are needed to reduce those barriers? What are some areas of success and support that they say they receive from the school?

4 In a rural school district in North Carolina, a local community Hispanic advocacy group provided monthly transportation to ML families to attend the district's school board meetings. Families were provided with opportunities to practice asking questions and to stand before the school board prior to their attendance. Over time, they became more comfortable with asking important questions about their child's education, services for ML students, and bilingual education programs. Do advocacy organizations for ML families exist in your community? How can you bridge the school-community space to support ML families in your school and district?

5 How do the concepts of *tequio, consejos,* and transcolonizing relate to your rural community? Do you see ways that ML families display these strengths in your school or community?

5

The Fourth Movement

Collaboration and Community

The Symphony as a Metaphor for Teamwork

A symphony thrives when dozens of instruments weave their distinct sounds into a balanced blend of melody, rhythm, and harmony. Every instrument contributes something vital to the whole, even the solitary tuba in Dvořák's *From the New World* symphony. Although its part is brief—the tuba appears only in the second movement—its deep resonance grounds the entire piece. Without it, the music would lose depth, richness, and structure. In some ways, the tuba player mirrors the reliable team member in a school setting—steady, unassuming, but essential.

Dvořák's professional success came from collaborations he fostered throughout his career by uplifting minoritized voices and traditions. As a teacher and director at the National Conservatory of Music in New York, Dvořák mentored female and Black American composers and incorporated Indigenous sounds into his work. As a result of his collaboration with diverse musical histories, identities, and knowledge, Dvořák created a uniquely "American" symphony.

DOI: 10.4324/9781003509875-5

Introduction

In this chapter, we examine the concept of collaboration and its significance both within rural schools and across community partners. This chapter is grounded in rural strengths and strength-based approaches to education. Specifically, we explore collaboration among rural educators to support and serve ML students and their families, as well as collaborative work and partnerships between rural community organizations and schools. These efforts have the potential to reimagine rural spaces in which educators no longer work in isolation, and schools can operate within a network of community support to serve their MLs.

As we have discussed throughout this book, rural schools are frequently geographically isolated, have small staffs who play multiple roles in schools, and have difficulty providing limited specialized services for MLs. These factors result in fragmented support for MLs. But not all rural schools are alike. For instance, in my state of North Carolina, one rural district that I work with has about 720 identified ML students and, in 2024, it had funding for only 2.5 FTE (full-time equivalent) English as a second language (ESL) teachers, making the ESL to ML student ratio about 1 for 288 MLs. About two hours' drive away, another district had a unique relationship with its business community to support immigrant MLs and could allocate more funding with a ratio of 1 ESL teacher to 40 MLs. Both districts have dual language immersion bilingual programs; however, the former district had one, while the latter district had six, with three at the elementary level. These examples demonstrate the diversity within and across districts that are equally considered rural.

At the same time, as described in Chapter 4, rural communities have unique strengths and "rural cultural wealth" that enable them to function in highly efficient ways. Some of those strengths include resourcefulness, kin-like relationships and networks, and rural ingenuity. Each rural school or district must know its strengths and how to leverage them for MLs. In fact, research indicates that targeted investments in rural schools *can* lead to higher student outcomes—especially when combined with strong educator practice and community engagement.

Part I: What It Is

In recent years, collaboration has become an increasingly important topic in education, emerging as a key area of research among scholars and a strategy among educators working with MLs. This is due in part to the challenging and changing context in which public schools and rural schools function. First, federal funding cuts now necessitate that all educators work as efficiently and collaboratively as possible. Recent federal policy priorities, and those in states such as North Carolina, are generating more school choice options for families. As funding flows away from public schools to fund these controversial initiatives, rural public schools will continue to experience financial constraints that may adversely affect the services they provide to MLs. Strategic collaboration in purposeful ways is one possible way to address financial pressures while meeting the needs of MLs and families.

Secondly, while there are some superheroes in education–highly-qualified teachers, dedicated leaders, bilingual staff who fully support MLs—no single person can realistically do everything or have all the answers when working with a dynamic and diverse ML student population. Rural educators, like all educators, face significant time constraints in their work, but rural educators are more isolated overall and perform a multitude of roles. So while collaboration is essential in all communities, urban, suburban, and small town, collaboration in rural schools is even more critical: it recognizes from the outset that rural educators must necessarily support one another and their students. In my work in rural schools, it is not unusual to hear that "one teacher is the entire ML department." Or that one ESL teacher serves multiple schools and travels long distances between schools to provide services. For rural educators who already work in close-knit and interdependent spaces, purposeful collaboration among teams of educators and community partners can therefore optimize support for rural MLs and families.

Third, collaboration can lead to novel and innovative solutions to educational problems that can be shared across teams. Rural innovation is a strength that responds to local needs and new ways to solve social and economic problems. For example, in a three-year professional development project that I led in rural north central Florida, collaboration emerged as *the* critical component that transformed education for rural ML students (Coady et al., 2022; Coady & Sorel, 2019). Our film, *Small Town Big Dreams*, depicts how one rural school professional development (PD) project, in which educators collaborated extensively, led to improved networks for rural MLs and to increased student achievement. A link to the film is in the resources section of this chapter.

Finally, rural schools cannot provide all of the resources that ML students and families may need, and every rural community is unique. Local solutions, such as language interpreters and culturally-knowledgeable advocates, must be identified locally for MLs, because those resources differ across rural communities. For instance, in one of our partner districts with rural Dual Language Immersion (rDLI) programs, families had access to mental health services and a strong neighborhood organization that networked with law enforcement and businesses. That community had a well-established and hardworking Latino neighborhood network. Another rDLI community had none of those networks, and so families had to travel significant distances for access to health and mental health services. Thus, aligning services through partnerships with the community can address local needs and uplift rural schools as hubs where information and resources can be shared.

Core Components of Effective Collaboration

Collaboration can occur spontaneously and often does in schools. Consider how many times you have mentioned to a colleague that you know an ML family who needs an interpreter or who has just relocated to the area and requires everyday household items like dishes, sheets, and towels. What happened? Did you reach further out to members of your family, school, or community to find those resources? Rural educators know how to network to find solutions through resourcefulness and the kin-like relationships that characterize many rural places. However, on a larger scale, purposeful collaboration, in which a team of educators shares goals, strengths, and networks, can be systematically transformative. The long-term objective is to create collaborations that are structural and built into the district-level leadership and school-level operations. These have longer-term benefits for when, for instance, a key person leaves the district or retires. Services and practices can continue for the ML students and families.

Scholars have identified several core components of effective collaboration. Here, I describe them as (a) a shared *purpose and relational trust* among educators; (b) expertise, skills, and leadership that are *distributed* across various school roles and members; and (c) educators learning *from and with* the community, particularly ML families. I describe these key ideas in the following sections. From my PD work in rural communities, I underscore these components as essential actions that are more than just theoretical ideas.

Relational Trust

Strong educator collaboration is rooted in **relational trust**, characterized by relationships among people who trust one another, are vulnerable to one another, and are interdependent. As Hargreaves (2007) reminds us, trust is the foundation of meaningful collaboration. When educators trust one another, they create professional cultures where colleagues are valued both personally and professionally, committed to their students' success, and open to honest dialogue—even disagreement—about evidence and data that can strengthen their teaching.

Scholars Bryk and Schneider examined collaboration among educators and the role of trust in collaboration. Their (2002) research highlights **relational trust** as a key resource for improving schools and student outcomes. They describe it as the "connective tissue" that unites educators, families, and communities around a shared commitment to children's learning and well-being (p. 144). Drawing on the concept of social capital (Coleman, 1988), Bryk and Schneider found that strong relational ties foster clear communication, mutual expectations, and a collective commitment to common goals. A collective commitment to common goals is similar to the shared vision discussed in Chapter 3 of this book. Notably, the authors emphasize that trust develops through vulnerability—when educators consciously act to reduce one another's uncertainty and demonstrate care and reliability in their daily interactions.

Trust cannot be built through a single PD session or educator team retreat. It emerges gradually through educators' consistent actions, transparent intentions, and the daily work of recognizing problems and innovating solutions together. Bryk and Schneider (2003) base their work on a ten-year study of over 400 elementary schools. Their work showed that high levels of trust encouraged voluntary collaboration among teachers, responsive leadership, and authentic partnerships with families—all of which strengthened school reform efforts. They also collected evidence from classroom observations, interviews, and community conversations to show how collaboration worked among educators. Their data demonstrated that trust is not just a desirable quality—it is *essential* for lasting school improvement.

According to the authors, relational trust operates across three interconnected levels: **intrapersonal**—shaped by each individual's background, beliefs, and past experiences—and **interpersonal**—developed through daily interactions and the shared culture of a school. This also includes a shared vision for ML students and the **organization**—reflected in broader outcomes such as stronger decision-making, innovation, and shared accountability. Individuals are central to collaboration, and who they (or we) are as educators shapes our beliefs and informs the kinds of interpersonal relationships we build. Relational trust grows from these layers of personal and collective interaction among teachers, leaders, families, and community members. It influences how educators interpret their responsibilities, view one another's intentions, and engage in collaborative problem-solving.

Schools with high relational trust are more likely to sustain educational improvement because educators share a moral and professional obligation to support one another to ensure high expectations and achievement among students and support their social and emotional development. This work is especially relevant to rural educators of ML students, because for rural schools, where community ties are often deep and personal, building relational trust is especially vital. This kind of collaboration allows teachers not only to support one another but also to challenge each other in ways that lead to real growth and improvement (p. 188). When teachers work together, they not only strengthen their professional practice but also honor the interconnected fabric of rural life. In so doing, they create schools in which collaboration, respect, and belonging form the foundation of equitable learning opportunities for all students.

Distributed Expertise

A second component of effective collaboration is the distribution of expertise. I especially gravitate to this characteristic of collaboration because I believe and am regularly reminded that all people in a team have unique expertise and life experiences to contribute to the group. For rural schools and educators, this shared or distributed expertise characterizes how many rural schools may already operate. In rural schools, as noted earlier, teachers and educators perform multifaceted roles and share their expertise freely with others for the collective good. In one of our rural partner school districts, for example, the secondary Spanish teacher took on the tasks of translating information for Spanish-speaking families. She had the expertise in language and the cultural background knowledge as a Latina to ensure that the information families received was linguistically and culturally relevant. She also became a technology expert—an area of great interest to her—and successfully introduced a Seal of Biliteracy in her local district, where the Spanish-speaking ML students acquired high levels of literacy in both English and Spanish.

Before participating in my rural ML PD project, where bilingualism and multilingualism were centered in the work of educators, she remarked that her "language learners seemed like ghosts" (Marichal et al., 2021, p. 53). During the PD, which involved a high degree of educator collaboration on projects and activities, she realized the importance of bilingualism and biliteracy development for the MLs. This is when she initiated the Seal of Biliteracy in her school. By reaching out to ML families, sharing her expertise, and collaborating with colleagues in distributed expertise, the ML students were able to graduate with Advanced Placement credit in Spanish and the Seal of Biliteracy on their high school diplomas.

A sole ESL teacher in a rural Wisconsin school district recently recounted how she created a network of supports and shared her expertise to identify resources for rural ML families. When she was asked how she leveraged linguistic resources in her community, she replied, "I don't have a magic wand," but used her insider relationships to identify someone in the community who had answers for families or who could identify solutions for them. Thus, building networks of resources within rural schools and communities for ML families is essential to ensure that families receive timely and useful communication and have access to information in their preferred languages. Even when rural educators, for instance, do not know or speak all of the languages of their students, someone in the community likely does. Relying on a network of support within or outside of the school is a key characteristic of rural schools and of distributed expertise, where all members' knowledge in the community is valued.

Unfortunately, some research on rural ML education reveals that the language, cultural knowledge, and networking skills of bilingual paraeducators or family liaison staff are undervalued or overlooked in rural schools (Coady et al., 2024; Reeves, 2023). For example, in her study of rural paraeducators, Reeves (2023) recounts the story of Manuela, a bilingual paraeducator who served students in a rural school district. Manuela moved to the area with her husband, who worked in a meatpacking plant. She became a bilingual paraeducator when her own children went to school. But her bilingualism and cultural knowledge were undervalued. In an interview, Manuela lamented,

> Honestly, this is something that hurts my feelings so much. Teachers should be respectful of us and treat everybody as the same. Many teachers they don't like some things just because we have, we have different ways to do stuff. And, I think that is one of the main things that every teacher has to have in their minds: different is okay.

We identified similar findings in our work in a rural North Carolina school with a large number of ML students. The district had several bilingual family liaisons who traveled between schools to support the ML students, interpreted at meetings, and worked with families by identifying resources (social, emotional, and material) that they needed. One bilingual family liaison staff member stated that educators frequently referred to them only as "the translator" and undervalued their skills in assisting families, and building community and networks to support ML students (Coady et al., 2024). Recognizing the strengths of bilingual educators and support staff signals significant agency for them to use their skills to support MLs, families, and educators. This is an example of recognizing diverse areas of expertise.

Distributed expertise is another feature of strong collaboration. Distributed expertise requires rethinking the traditional role of the school leader, often the principal, in favor of identifying expertise from across all educators within the school and members of the community. Principals are frequently the outward-facing image of the school and often act as 'boundary spanners' between institutions or community organizations and families (Ishimaru, 2013). They establish partnerships with community agencies, churches, and local businesses, serving as conduits for strong collaborative networks both outside and within the school walls. Yet at the same time, other members of the school and community can use their networking and expertise to establish partnerships and relationships. In other words, boundary spanning can be undertaken by people other than the traditional school leader.

Highly skilled leaders, including teacher-leaders and advocates, can build a culture of collaboration and community with ML families by ensuring that they are represented in school events and activities. For example, one rural principal of an rDLI program encouraged ML families to create their own Parent Teacher Association (PTA) so that they could be equally informed about school events and participate in school activities. The bilingual PTA was open to everyone, and bilingual families offered to interpret for English-speaking families who wished to attend. In the bilingual PTA, ML families were able to contribute to the school's vision using their knowledge of the rural community and the school. This example illustrates the work of a school principal who encouraged distributed expertise by adopting an additive approach to family engagement, ensuring that

ML families were heard, seen, and actively involved in her rural elementary school.

School leaders who have bilingual and multicultural skills in the school and community are exceptionally important in rural settings. In the context of bilingual education programs, such as rDLI programs, Menken and Solorza (2015) describe how principals can serve as "linchpins" of DLI programs, either subverting or promoting bilingualism and bilingual education, particularly in times of restrictive language policy. As current federal policies continue to de-emphasize diversity, equity, and inclusion efforts, as well as the use of official English under Executive Order 14224, these pressures can challenge the very existence of highly successful dual language bilingual education programs. Indeed, a rural district where I worked recently (in early 2026) announced the abrupt, end-of-school year closure of 9 rDLI programs. While the rationale for these closures was not clearly articulated, ML families were left without agency or input into the decision-making process.

A new educational leader who lacks knowledge of bilingual education and expertise in affirming and networking with ML and bilingual families can leave bilingual programs vulnerable to low enrollment, attrition, and closure. Rural school leaders can work within the concept of distributed leadership, with expert bilingual educators, family liaison staff, ESL teachers, and para-educators to build their own expertise in bilingualism and ML family inclusion. With distributed expertise, teachers, aides, ML families, and community members contribute to the functioning of rural schools in different yet equally valued ways. In short, everyone's knowledge—including that of ML families and groups that are often invisible—is valued, and their contributions to the community are a key condition for collaboration.

Learning From and With the Community

The third component of effective collaboration involves the school as a learning space that not only reflects the community's diverse members but also learns from them, drawing on their backgrounds, experiences, languages, races, and ethnicities. When school members—teachers, leaders, staff—learn from the local rural community and incorporate local knowledge and resources into the school functioning and curriculum, schools can be transformative spaces that disrupt inequities and inequalities. The idea is to prioritize local place-conscious educational practices, including language and cultural knowledge, into the school itself. Does the school reflect local demographics? Local knowledge and ways of being? And local languages and cultures?

One seminal example of a relationship that tapped into the community's knowledge and functioning was in a seminal study conducted by Moll and colleagues. Moll et al. (1992) conducted an ethnographic exploration of Mexican-American households in Arizona. They sought to understand the deep reservoirs of cultural and intellectual capital embedded in families' everyday practices. The researchers approached this work not as evaluators but as learners. They documented the social networks, work histories, and problem-solving strategies that immigrant and ML families used to navigate daily life.

What the researchers found directly contradicted deficit-based views about working-class and immigrant families. Rather than lacking educational resources, these households possessed sophisticated bodies of knowledge—mechanical, agricultural, entrepreneurial, linguistic, and social—that were simply invisible to schools. For example, one family's carpentry and home renovation skills became a culturally responsive resource for lessons in measurement, geometry, and design. In another instance, families' agricultural and gardening knowledge informed science lessons about plant biology and ecology, grounding abstract concepts in tangible, local experiences. This aligns with rural place-based education (Corbett, 2020), in which local communities are sites where local knowledge is unearthed and elevated, rather than imported from outside the community.

The practices in Moll et al.'s 1992 study did more than make learning relevant—they redefined the teacher's role. Teachers became ethnographers of their students' worlds, blurring the line between "home" and "school." The classroom became a space where community knowledge wasn't merely included for surface-level cultural activities but treated as a legitimate, rigorous foundation for curriculum design. Moll et al.'s work demonstrates how educators can learn *from* the community and how knowledge is local, varied, and derived from multiple sources.

Lucas and Villegas extend this concept by emphasizing *linguistically responsive schooling*—the idea that students' language practices are not barriers to learning but assets. Rural communities often include multilingual families, dialect diversity, and culturally specific communication patterns. Linguistically responsive educators intentionally design instruction that honors these linguistic repertoires, helping students navigate both their local and academic worlds. By valuing students' home languages and discourse styles, teachers affirm identity and strengthen relationships between families and schools. Together, linguistically responsive schooling and funds of knowledge theory capture the notion of "learning from and within the community" as both an ethical stance and a pedagogical strategy. Rather than importing external models of "good teaching," educators, leaders, and school staff become researchers and collaborators within their communities—learning *from* and *with* local families. The result is a symbiotic ecosystem of knowledge where classroom inquiry reflects the lived realities of rural life.

In education, teamwork isn't just about agreement—it is about active mentorship and listening. Dvořák's music teacher saw potential in his work that others ignored. Dvořák, in turn, amplified unheard voices: that's what a team should do. Building collaborative teams of educators that meet the needs of rural ML students and families is predicated upon relational trust, shared and distributed expertise that includes members of the community and ML families, and learning from and with the community. These characteristics tap into rural cultural wealth, rural resourcefulness, familism, ingenuity, and community unity. Importantly, these ideas unearth nontraditional forms of knowledge, minoritized languages, and nondominant cultures to redistribute power and relationships both within the school and across the community.

Part II: What It Looks Like

What does this work—collaborative teams, or orchestral groups that connect rural schools and communities for ML families—look like in practice? Next, I provide examples of how rural collaborations can function optimally to support MLs. They are based on decades of experience working in rural communities with MLs and families, as well as research I have conducted with rural MLs in the U.S. and other countries such as South Africa and Ireland. In the following sections, I include school-based team efforts and community-driven partnerships with schools. I further propose that university-level partnerships with pre-service teachers can be fostered as an added resource for rural districts. These are illustrative examples that, ideally, spark rural educators' ideas and how these can be adapted to meet local community and demographic needs. I describe these as different systems levels of collaboration, beginning with school-based collaborative teams through co-teaching and shared expertise and planning with grade- and content-area educators. Moving outside of the school, I describe rural educator networks through PLCs and educator-family collaborative partnerships. Then, at the school-community level, I describe community-driven models of collaboration that include rural advocacy groups and university partnerships.

School-Based Collaborative Teams

Collaboration through Co-teaching

An important way that educators can collaborate is at the classroom level. Teachers can co-teach in various ways, but most importantly, how they choose to co-teach should reflect key principles of collaboration, described earlier as relational trust, distributed expertise, and learning from each other. Collaborating for instructional purposes, such as co-teaching, can be a powerful approach to optimizing rural resources for ML students.

In their book, *Co-teaching for English Learners: A Guide to Collaborative Planning, Instruction, Assessment, and Reflection*, Dove and Honigsfeld (2018) describe six flexible collaborative structures teachers can use, depending on the goals for teaching, the time that educators have, and the classroom needs, specifically the learning needs of ML students with different language proficiency levels or home languages. Educators should collaborate for MLs across planning, implementation, and reflection after the lesson is delivered. The authors identify six different collaborative, co-teaching approaches:

1. **One Teach, One Observe**
   One teacher leads the lesson; the other observes specific student behaviors, language use, or engagement patterns. This helps collect data on ML students and identify additional supports they may need.
2. **One Teach, One Assist**
   One teacher instructs while the other circulates, supporting individuals or small groups who need clarification or additional help. This approach is often used when starting new co-teaching teams.
3. **Station Teaching**
   The class is divided into small groups; each teacher leads one station while others work independently. This works well when lessons are differentiated by language proficiency level or skill development (listening, speaking, reading, and writing). This can work for MLs when stations are guided, and students know exactly what to do at the station through modeling, visuals, anchor charts, and paired activities.
4. **Parallel Teaching**
   The class is split into two groups, and each teacher teaches the same content simultaneously. Like stations, this allows ML students to interact in small groups. ML students can be scaffolded through repeated exposure to concepts and content, and teachers can pace instruction at the rate at which MLs can process language and work through content.
5. **Alternative Teaching**
   One teacher works with a small group for targeted instruction while the other manages the larger group. This works well with pre-teaching material or building background knowledge about a new concept, re-teaching material that students did not master in a prior lesson, or extending learning by deepening and/or extending concepts.
6. **Team Teaching**
   Both teachers share equal responsibility in delivering content and language instruction simultaneously. Team teaching requires teachers to be balanced in their delivery. This approach requires strong trust between teachers and planning to ensure that both teachers are in sync.

In order to most efficiently engage in these collaborative structures or models, educators need to work together to build relational trust. As I noted earlier, relational trust occurs over time and with time, when educators can work together purposefully to identify problems and innovate solutions.

The aforementioned models further underscore the collaborative principle of distributed expertise and relational trust among educators. Vintan and Gallagher (2019) examined co-teaching in small rural communities and found that it was challenging. They found that rural educators lacked sufficient time to plan and faced additional challenges, including limited training, technology, and tools needed to facilitate collaboration. Educators who aim to co-teach across any of these models must honor each other's time and commit to co-planning and co-reflecting in a timely manner.

Another way rural school districts with limited resources can collaborate is through shared expertise within grade-level teams or content-area team meetings. As one secondary content teacher remarked to me recently, "I don't need more team planning in my content area, I need more time with the ESL specialist or the EC [Exceptional Child] specialist to help me support the MLs in my classroom." In my teacher education program in Multilingual Education, I repeatedly emphasize to my students that they need to provide the language expertise that teachers may not already have. That means finding allies across grades and content areas and asking to attend a monthly grade-level meeting or team content meeting. Individual students' needs can be swiftly addressed through regular, open communication.

These collaborations can lead to shifts in the instructional model for ML students. For instance, content teachers often lament that the ML students are pulled out of the classroom to go to ESL during a critical content lesson. One possibility is that educators together ask that the ESL teacher push into classrooms to provide support for ML students during content instruction rather than pulling ML students out. As noted earlier, however, this requires some planning in advance for the ESL teacher to understand the content objectives, align language objectives for the ML students at different language proficiency levels, and bring in differentiated graphic organizers, bilingual glossaries,

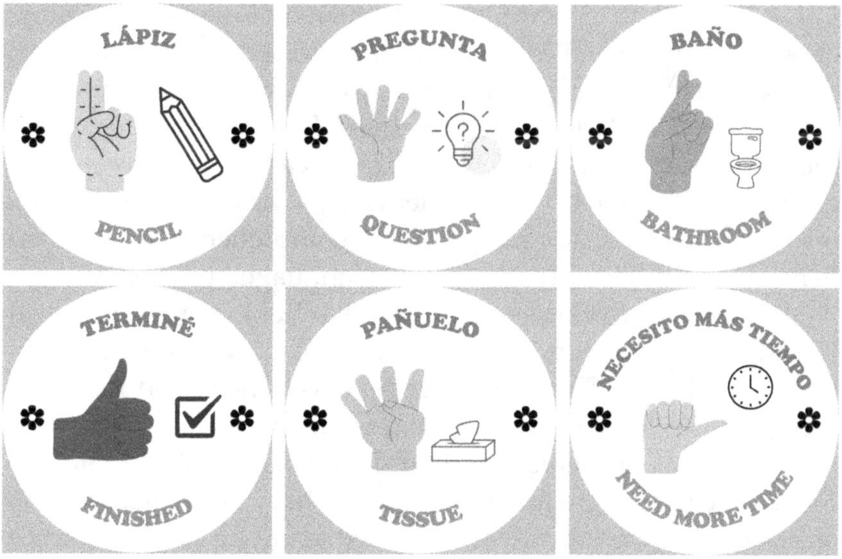

FIGURE 5.1 Multilingual-multimodal communication chart. Image by the author.

visual aids, realia, and other language-learning supports for MLs in the content area. It also requires that the school rethink the ESL teachers' work and scheduling. Shared or distributed expertise in these classrooms can support both teachers and ML students. For instance, the ESL language specialists can provide or create parallel anchor charts in MLs' home languages for the content-area classroom. Figure 5.1 is an image of multilingual-multimodal communication charts in Spanish, English, and sign language in a third-grade bilingual mathematics classroom.

The example shows that collaboration between content and specialist teachers can result in ML students' improved understanding of classroom procedures and routines, language transfer (e.g., cognates across languages they use or know), and more culturally responsive classroom instruction and management.

Collaboration across Roles of Educators

At the rural school level, creating a structure for purposeful planning and solutions is essential. Brainstorming among language specialists, such as ESL teachers and family liaisons, and general educators is critical to aligning services for MLs. For example,

ESL teachers and general educators, such as grade-level teams of teachers in elementary schools or math teachers in secondary schools, can meet weekly or biweekly to co-plan lessons and integrate content and language objectives. Both sets of educators—the ESL faculty and the general education faculty—should discuss the needs of ML students and ways to differentiate instruction to make language content comprehensible ("comprehensible input") for MLs at different language proficiency levels.

Recently, I worked with a rural school district in North Carolina that had seen a 10% year-over-year increase in the number of rural MLs. The superintendent was concerned that there were insufficient ESL teachers to meet the needs of the growing number of ML students, and that there was realistically no way to increase funding to hire more ESL teachers. He recognized that all educators across the district needed to have a stake in the academic progress and learning of ML students. The superintendent decided that the school leaders—in this case, principals, assistant principals, senior coaching staff, and ESL faculty—needed to have similar entry points to support MLs, and a shared vision and collaboration. Working together, he envisioned two full-day PD events where all leaders learned language principles for working with MLs, creating a shared vision for MLs (see Chapter 3), and collaborating for MLs and families.

This rural district was geographically large in area, but the district office buildings were located in a small town. On the first day, the district sent buses to the various schools to pick up the educators and transport them to the central district offices for the PD. The need for educators to be together, an easy request for urban or suburban educators, was essential for the district leaders to begin forming collaborative partnerships within and across schools. In particular, the district leaders aimed to align elementary, middle, and high schools in articulating support for MLs across the three settings.

Working with the ESL team, we generated examples of how ESL teachers could collaborate with grade and content-area teams. This was onelevel of collaboration between language specialists such as ESL teachers and content-area teachers. At the district-community level, the district leadership team forged strong partnerships between the district, local community colleges, and teacher education institutions. Collaborations between university partners and rural districts created a structural pipeline for educators to complete field placements, practica, and internships in the district. This addressed the persistent and pressing issue of identifying and retaining teachers in rural communities (Rhinesmith et al., 2023).

In a rural community in North Carolina, the ML lead teacher for the district organized a regional ("Sandhills Region") off-site meeting for colleagues from across several districts to meet, identify concerns, share resources, and build a collaborative network. The ML lead also invited local community organizations, such as the Islamic Center, which also operated a food bank, staff from the state's free Legal Aid clinic, and former ML students who had graduated from the district and continued to serve as mentors for ML students within the district. The networking from nearby districts helped build a regional rural network. This example demonstrates the pivotal role of ML and ESL staff in networking and collaboration, and how rural networks can be established.

Rural Collaboration with Virtual Communities of Practice

As the use of technology becomes increasingly ubiquitous in education and learning, rural communities can benefit from forming professional relationships within and across their communities. However, not all rural communities have equal access to these technologies. On the one hand, technological tools have made collaborations easier and more convenient; however, they don't always work effectively for rural communities. There remains in the U.S. a distinct "digital divide" (Greiman et al., 2023). The "digital divide" refers to inequities in internet access among demographic groups. It also refers to geographic barriers (e.g., remote mountain communities or small islands) that lack either the infrastructure or a service provider to access the internet. On a remote rural island for instance, even a minor weather disruption can knock out the internet for hours or days. Even though educators frequently state that they wish to mitigate a sense of isolation and work together in the same space, geography, transportation, time, and financial resources can remain barriers to this. Thus, technology can be helpful for educators of rural MLs, but it is not consistently accessible or even available.

Through technology, however, educators can form a network of support to mitigate geographic, social, and professional isolation. In prior PD work with educators of MLs in rural north Florida, participants in my PD began the program using an online learning platform for coursework and professional discussion groups. Within six months, the teachers, leaders, and counselors asked to reframe the PD to include time for physical interaction and learning together. As a group, we honored that request while retaining an online component of the work for educators to network and share. The use of technology helped mitigate the feeling of isolation. Hybrid or Virtual Communities of Practice (VCoPs) can create networks of rural educators who share goals and establish mutual support. This can be especially affirming for educators who may be the only person in that district role, such as a rural ESL teacher or mobile rural school counselor.

Communities of Practice (CoPs), according to Wenger (1998), are groups of people who share a concern, a set of problems, or a passion for a topic. Among educators, CoP members deepen their knowledge and expertise through ongoing interaction. Vurtual COPs are conducted entirely online, whereas hybrid CoPs, as described earlier, can use both in-person and online formats. For rural educators, a VCoP can be an essential for professional growth and collaboration, particularly when geographic isolation limits access to formal networks or resources. Through shared practice and dialogue, rural educators can co-construct solutions tailored to their unique contexts, exchange culturally responsive strategies, and sustain collective learning despite limited institutional support.

In our online PD with CoPs, educators engaged in book clubs and discussions on immigration, bilingualism, and education for minoritized students, sharing resources and connecting their book club readings with real-time issues in their rural communities. In this PD, CoP members read nonfiction narrative books about immigration, and they connected with those stories through counternarratives (Golombek et al., 2022). The members could choose from adult novels, memoirs, or fiction, and young adult novels. One participant, who was a rural instructional aide, was so engaged with the list of books that she decided to read them all. Some of the books that educators read in the CoP book club, adult novels, included:

- *The Same Sky*, Amanda Eyre Ward
- *Enrique's Journey*, Sonia Nazario
- *The Barbarian Nurseries*, Héctor Tobar
- *Spare Parts: Four Undocumented Teenagers, One Ugly Robot, and the Battle for the American Dream*, Joshua Davis
- *In the Country We Love: My Family Divided*, Diane Guerrero and Michelle Burford

As educators engaged in online book club VCoPs, they connected readings to their rural communities and learned about the experiences of immigrants and MLs' families. As part of their learning, the educators visited some of their ML families' homes. They engaged in conversations with them about their experiences as MLs and their community work.

In a VCoP with educators in a rural health initiative, Dickson et al. (2024) examined a VCoP in a remote rural community. They conducted focus groups with 13 participants. They found that the VCoP was overwhelmingly positive. Some of the primary outcomes included an increased sense of belonging and connection, a reduced sense of isolation, opportunities to exchange new ideas, and a strong sense of collaboration. For instance, one participant stated,

> To be able to sit and have somebody that's been a mini expert in an area and say, "Look at this. This is what I've experienced. This is what a great resource is." This is what we are doing in [my town]. Even though you guys are down the road from us, we have similar situations. I may not have the exact tools that you guys have already been utilizing (male urban participant).
>
> *(Dickson et al., 2024, p. 6)*

Educators can establish VCoPs through shared professional networks, such as utilizing state and national organizations. For instance, annual educator conferences with state Departments of Public Instruction for MLs, or national or regional bilingual education associations (National Association for Bilingual Education, Carolina Association for Bilingual Education) are an established network that can be tapped to bring rural educators together. Educators can use their shared network to host a rural ML educator VCoP with book clubs, monthly sharing-space meetings, or presentations with Q&A for other educators to adapt to their rural communities.

ML Parent Organizing and School District Collaboration

In Chapter 4, I described a key principle for rural ML education: recentering families in rural ML family engagement. It is important to reiterate here that collaboration between educators and ML families is essential, and it truly takes a team of educators who care; that is, no single member of the school community should be responsible for ML family engagement. Educators can collaborate to identify families' languages, cultures, resources, needs, and ways to bring them into the school community through shared information and leadership roles.

In my work on a multiple-site case study of rural rDLI programs, I examined the ecosystem within which these programs operate. I sought out how rural schools networked with community advocates and agencies to support rural MLs and their families. One neighborhood Latino advocacy group in a fringe rural school district built engagement and advocacy efforts with Latino parents over a three-decade period. The director, Alissa (pseudonym) described the goals of her organization: to assist Latino parents in understanding (a) how schools in the U.S. work; (b) how the leadership structures, such as school boards and advisory groups, shaped the schools and programs that their children participated in; and (c) ways that parents could have a collective voice in decision-making roles in the school district.

As she began her work in the late 1990s, Alissa initially acted as an interpreter at school board meetings, bringing families to the meetings and working with them to model and practice speaking before the school board. Over time, her organization trained community advocates to build community education networks for their children and to serve on advisory boards. With her assistance, ML families were provided safe spaces to ask questions about their children's education, schools, and services. They further taught parents leadership communication strategies through modeling and group activities. They also provided transportation for families to attend monthly school board meetings, a practice that continues.

Over time, parents became more comfortable asking questions of the school board and conveying their needs and concerns to its members. Latino parents began to set district goals and participate in strategic planning, sharing power with other families and district leaders. Working from families' needs emphasizes that collaboration should begin with family and community priorities rather than imposing the school's agenda on ML families.

Fotonovelas as Culturally and Linguistically Responsive Family Support Materials

In much of my prior work with schools and families, I have created and used locally-informed graphic novels, called *fotonovelas* in Spanish, for bilingual families. These print materials derive from the work of the Rural Women's Health Project (RWHP.org), a community health advocacy with rural Spanish-speaking families that I have worked with for over two decades.

The goal of the fotonovela is to provide accessible, relevant information to ML families; they are used for reflection, role modeling, and empowerment within minoritized communities. Fotonovelas are created using dialogue and images of people who resemble community members. The fotonovelas should stimulate conversations in which families, parents, or others identify a shared problem they face and propose a solution using the expertise or knowledge of a member of their community. These materials have a long history of cultural and linguistic responsiveness. The idea is to utilize these materials and have families "pay them forward" by supporting someone else, perhaps another newcomer or ML family, in the community.

Although they originate from lay workers in the healthcare community (e.g., Unger et al., 2013), I have adapted the novelas for use with rural Spanish-speaking Latino families in education. Some topics in the education fotonovelas include *"No sé inglés, ¿qué hago?"* [I don't know English, what do I do?]. This fotonovela serves as a guide for non-English-speaking parents to communicate with their child's school. An example is shown in Figure 5.2.

FIGURE 5.2 Fotonovela: No sé inglés, ¿Qué hago? Produced by the author.

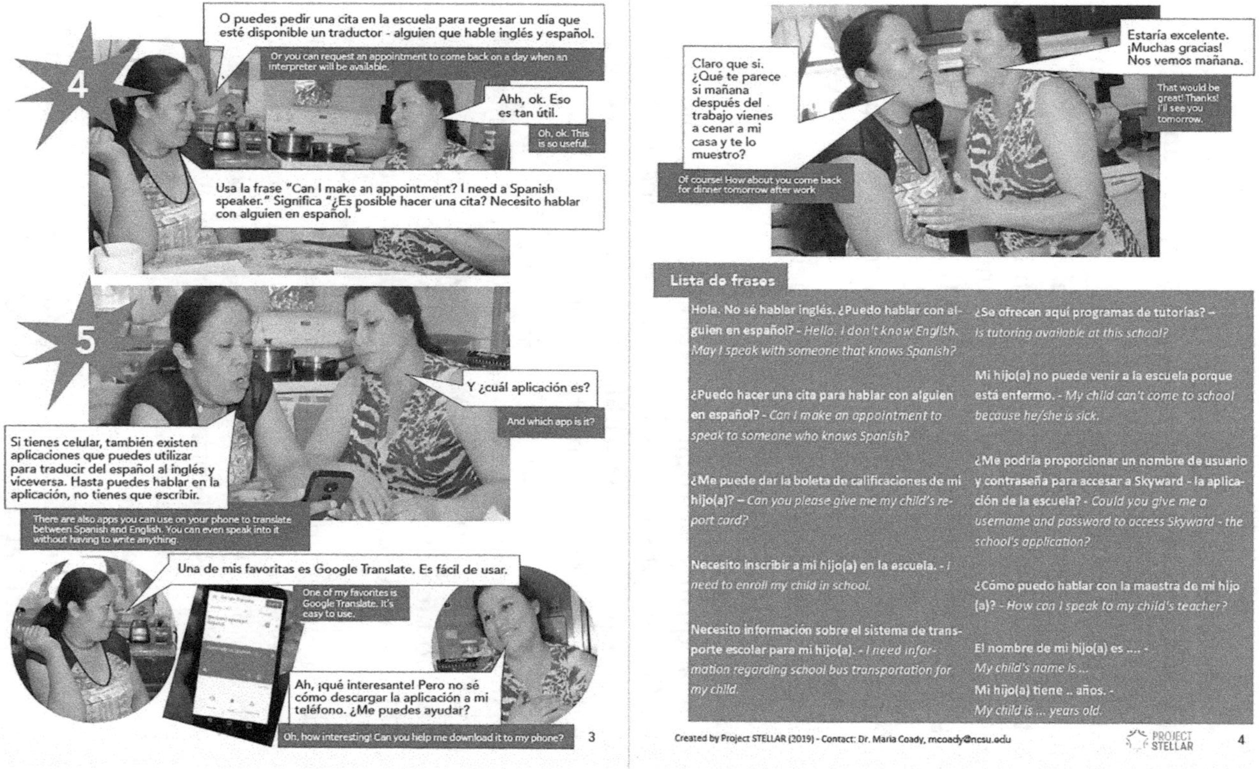

FIGURE 5.2 (continued)

Another is how to read the report card, and a third fotonovela assists parents in understanding what a parent-teacher conference is about and what to expect. These fotonovelas were developed in response to families' needs. They were used by teachers, school leaders, and family advocates to support families within their rural communities.

Collaboration between ML families and schools can alter communication structures: rather than relying solely on English newsletters and one-way meetings, multilingual parent leaders can co-design workshops for other Spanish-speaking parents, develop materials, and engage community and family networks. A strong school-family collaboration encourages families to lead in their language and on their terms. Moreover, multilingual families can serve as co-investigators in school improvement—not merely recipients of translated materials.

Community Connector Roles

An essential quality of rural communities is the unique ways they function and the close kin-like relationships, such as family or "familism," that exist within the community. People know one another and identify ways to remain close and support one another, particularly in times of need. Rural schools play critical roles in the functioning of rural communities. They are hubs of activity, ranging from weekly movie nights and community food banks to funeral homes and health clinics. The space itself, as a public shared venue, is irreplaceable for community functioning and well-being. Thus, to the extent that these spaces truly reflect the language and cultural resources of the community, as safe spaces for people to visit, they hold promise of reversing stereotypes and biases that too often characterize non-English-speaking families. Rural community events provide opportunities for staff, educators, and paraeducators to serve as connectors by attending church, sporting, cultural, harvest festival, fair, and library book events.

Rural teachers describe how they often interact with families in their community at soccer events or church services. Bilingual paraeducators or Spanish-language teachers, if available at the school, translate materials and facilitate informal two-way communication. The work of two scholars, Jenelle Reeves and Stephanie Oudghiri, examines how paraeducators are positioned in rural communities and the essential role they play in ensuring that ML students and families remain informed and connected. Paraeducators are frequently members of the ML community themselves, and they also live in the communities that they serve. Their insider knowledge is irreplaceable and a highly valuable skill. However, they too often feel underappreciated for their language skills and for the time they spend with families, listening to their needs, and identifying solutions to support their children in school (Coady et al., 2024).

In rural South Florida, the bilingual school in Immokalee serves farmworker students and families. The principal fostered purposeful, strong relationships with families by implementing programs such as Saturday Camps and after-school study halls, enabling students to remain at school while their parents worked. As a former child of a farmworker family, she understood—from her lived experiences—the needs of these families and the ways the school could build supports and serve them. She stated, "The community helped me ... and this is a way for me to give back." These sentiments are shared across rural communities, which operate as a tight-knit family.

Family, Community, and University Partnerships

In 2005, I began teaching ESL in a rural community in north central Florida. The industry base consisted of plant nurseries and hay bales, and many families had relocated to the community for employment opportunities. Initially, I organized weekly ESL classes for adults at a rural public library. The librarians were extremely helpful regarding the program and enthusiastic about encouraging patrons to visit the public library to access books, computers, and language-learning services. They assisted me in reserving two spaces each week: one for the adult ESL classes and another for student volunteers, who worked with children on homework and in second language development and literacy activities.

The ESL class was functional English-based, meaning the goal was to assist families in accessing language and services that they needed in everyday life. We worked together to complete bank account applications, doctor office visit forms, and practiced speaking on cell phones, where there are no visual cues for language, to order pizzas. This work continued for about three years, during which I gained a greater footing in the rural community and learned, from parents and educators, that children lacked books at home and needed more time for reading. The Migrant Education Program (MEP) staff, who visited farmworker families in their homes, confirmed that the children had limited access to print materials and to home reading.

The library-based ESL program subsequently took on a new direction. While working with my university's undergraduate preservice teacher students and the MEP program, which serves migratory children and families employed in agriculture, fishing, or dairy, I designed a mobile reading facilitation program featuring bilingual books. The program was called *Libros de Familia* (Family Books) (Coady & Moore, 2010). Using community and professional networks, I established a process to connect with families through the MEP program coordinators. We visited the homes of ML families and met with them to learn about their children, their educational experiences, and the topics their children enjoyed reading about. I obtained permission from the families for my volunteer students and me to bring bilingual books to their homes and read with their children each week.

I wrote and obtained a small grant and purchased approximately $5,000 in bilingual print books, ranging in ranging in reading complexity from picture books to young adult literature from picture books to young adult literature. The books were culturally relevant to the community I served and reflected the array of languages and cultural backgrounds of the students. My volunteer students paired up and made weekly visits to families' homes. Each week, the pair of student volunteers came to my university office and selected books for children to read at home. At least one of the two students was bilingual, able to speak and read some Spanish. The pair drove to a family home and spent 60–90 minutes reading books with a child. All the families resided in rural communities, located between 15 and 30 miles from the university. It often took the student volunteers as long to get to the home as it did to spend time with the children! After reading with the children and engaging in conversations about the story, and often conducting follow-up literacy activities with the children at home, the student volunteers left the book(s) for the children to re-read during the week. They returned the following week with new books and reading activities.

As the project coordinator, I organized bilingual books, engaged and met families during initial and subsequent visits, ensured that student volunteers had gas money to travel to homes, and followed up. We planned for both the start-of-semester activities and the final visit. The final visit was essential to plan, because the children were distraught when the volunteers did not return. Thus, I learned to schedule a closing meeting where the children and student volunteers could bid each other farewell. I ran the *Libros de Familia* project for almost a decade, achieving significant positive outcomes and creating lasting memories between the preservice teachers and ML students and families.

There were three critical outcomes from this work. First, the student volunteers established strong, trusting relationships with the ML children and their families. The relationships formed a basis for other supports and insights that we gained from the community. We learned, for instance, that many of the children lacked access to dental services and care. As a result, I established a way to bring children to regional, sliding-scale dental services. The district had emergency funds to assist families in paying for necessary emergency dental care. The student volunteers learned about the lives of the children they would later teach, and several eventually became school leaders and principals in bilingual schools in the state. In other words, the learning from this project had a long-term impact on educators, families, and ML students.

A second outcome was that the parents or caregivers themselves, some of whom had limited print literacy skills, also learned to read or decode bilingually. This "spontaneous biliteracy development" emerged from parents observing our shared reading practices and engaging in reading with their children using bilingual books. Spanish-print literate adults acquired the skills to decode English-language books. This was not a planned outcome but rather a natural phenomenon among bilingual individuals who contrast across two languages when they encounter the script and receive visual cues in the text.

Finally, we observed that the children were reading more often—of course—and wanted to keep the books to read repeatedly. This was important because migrant-background children move frequently to follow seasonal harvests. When the project, sadly, ended, we purchased small cases and gave all of the books away to the families to keep when they moved to a new community. Both access to bilingual books for ML children and shared reading made a difference in their desire to read before and after their participation in the project, I can safely say that both access to bilingual books for bilingual, ML children and shared, supported reading made a difference in their desire to read and share their reading with others.

In the *Libros de Familia* project, the MEP, schools, bilingual ML families, and university faculty and student volunteers collaborated—each playing a distinct role—to provide high-quality, bilingual reading materials and support for rural ML students. It was a metaphoric symphony of instruments. We cobbled together funding, found convenient times to meet, addressed the needs of rural ML families in their own communities and homes, and leveraged our shared bilingual resources.

Indicators of Successful Collaboration

As is evident in this chapter, collaboration can take many forms, and ultimately, strong collaborations are based on the key principles of relational trust, distributed expertise, and learning from and with the community. Importantly, each rural community has its own networks, culture of familism, and community wealth. How can we determine if collaborations are successful? One way is through increased participation among all stakeholders, including ML families and their children, community advocacy organizations, university partnerships with student placement options in the district, and retention of ML staff. Bilingual paraeducators and family liaison staff should feel included and trusted for their expertise. You and your colleagues could create self-reflection checklists to gauge the various levels, as outlined in this chapter, at which collaborations can take place: among classroom teachers, school educators and staff, schools and district personnel, and rural communities agencies.

Conclusion

In rural education, collaboration is not a "program" or another thing to do. Rather, it's a social infrastructure that sustains ML students' and families' belonging and visibility. Collaboration is a series of actions and activities. Collaboration can occur at the classroom, school, family, and community levels. Just as a symphony's success relies on each section's awareness of the others, effective collaboration in schools grows from mutual respect and responsiveness. Teachers form the orchestra. ESL specialists harmonize with content teachers, while family liaisons, leaders, and counselors engage families to support multilingual learners and sustain the school's rhythm. Collaboration is about tuning to the same key.

Successful collaboration is based on key principles of relational trust, distributed expertise, and learning from and with the community. The community encompasses all members, including newcomers, non-English speakers, established ML families, and advocacy groups. This chapter provided examples of how rural educators can use and adapt collaborative principles to their local schools and communities.

DISCUSSION QUESTIONS FOR CHAPTER 5

1 What different types of collaboration take place in your school and district? Are these collaborations within the school, between the school and the community, and/or inclusive of ML families? What types of collaboration are "missing" in ways that would support the academic learning and social well-being of your ML students?
2 Rural schools are frequently described as low-resourced and low-funded. How is it related to structural inequities and inequalities in school funding? How can this descriptor be challenged to include the school's rural cultural strengths, such as collaboration and familism, distributed expertise, and rural ingenuity?
3 As teachers who serve ML students and families, what types of collaborative teaching, as described in this chapter, could be innovated in your school to support ML students? Who would be involved in the scheduling and planning to pilot one of the six types of co-teaching?
4 Consider the Virtual Community of Practice. How applicable and valuable is a VCoP in your rural community? What benefits can you anticipate by bringing together rural educators for MLs across your district, region, or state? What infrastructure, materials, and human resources would you need to implement a VCoP?
5 How could the fotonovela be used in your district or school? What other topics for fotonovelas does your district need to support rural ML families?

6

An Action Plan for Rural Multilingual Learner Education

Introduction

You are integral to your rural community. How we proceed in our shared space can either limit or extend possibilities of each other's lives, as well as those of our multilingual learners (ML) students and their families. Throughout this book, we have explored four educational movements or principles, essential for creating equal, equitable, and effective education for rural MLs and their families. These include Principle 1: Representation and Belonging, Principle 2: Shared Vision, Principle 3: Recentering ML Families, and Principle 4: Collaborative Teams to Connect Rural Schools and Communities for MLs.

Like the four movements in Dvořák's *From the New World* symphony, each principle contributes to the harmonious whole—a comprehensive approach to supporting rural ML students. For Dvořák to have been successful and to have created a uniquely American symphony meant that Thurber's vision for inclusive education, Burleigh's expertise in Black spiritual music, and Dvořák's study of Indigenous histories, knowledges, and sounds were brought together in new and transformational ways.

This analogy conveys that, even in the earliest moments of our country's history as the United States of America, diversity

DOI: 10.4324/9781003509875-6

and inclusion have been at the very core of our history, the deepest display of what it means to be an American. Indigenous tribes, Black Americans, and linguistically and ethnically diverse immigrants are the lifeblood of the U.S. Ironically, Dvořák, an outsider to the U.S. and deeply homesick for his native country, returned after his contract ended in 1895. Yet as an outsider, Dvořák fully understood the relationship between people and the land they inhabit and was anxious to return to his own roots. His experiences as a young Czech musician influenced the development of his compositional style. He knew that a symphony from America had to be based on the American story, not on those of another nation or people.

These unlikely but essential events wove together to create a new tapestry of music for generations to come. Dvořák's student, William Arms Fisher, later set the Second Movement to lyrics in the famous *"Goin' Home,"* a tune you are likely familiar with familiar with, often played at the funerals of important statespersons (Lewis, 2020). Dvořák's 9th Symphony, *From the New World*, inspires a message of unity and transcends any singular culture.

Review of the Four Movements

In Chapter 1, I introduced the demographic realities facing rural schools today: increasing linguistic diversity, persistent funding disparities, and the urgent need for educators who understand both rurality and multilingual education. Rural ML students, like all rural children, deserve equal resources. MLs also merit equitable, language-responsive programs, practices, and spaces. Equal and equitable are not necessarily at odds. A starting point for rural schools is to advocate for equal funding for rural schools relative to metropolitan counterparts to provide high-quality education for all students, with teachers, leaders, and staff who are adequately compensated and supported with the resources they need to perform their jobs. The symphonic metaphor invited us to view education as a collaborative, multifaceted endeavor in which every instrument—every educator, family member, and community partner—plays an essential role in the success of ML students.

The First Movement, found in Chapter 2 of this volume, involves building a sense of belonging through representation and translanguaging for rural ML and their families. This chapter is essential, foundational work. In this chapter, I discussed how when ML students see their languages, cultures, and identities reflected in the air, in the halls, and on the walls of their schools, they develop a stronger sense of belonging and an affirmation of who they are as individuals and members of the rural classroom, school, and community. This sense of belonging is not merely a feel-good concept—research consistently demonstrates its connection to academic achievement, social-emotional well-being, and long-term educational outcomes. As educators, we want every student to belong and to feel it. We can take deliberate steps that ensure our ML students belong in our classrooms, schools, and communities. The chapter offers numerous visual examples of the representation of ML students' identities and knowledge in rural schools.

The Second Movement, located in Chapter 3, examined a shared vision among educators who work with MLs—the collective north star that guides educators toward common goals for ML students. Drawing on the example of Jeannette Thurber, whose inclusive vision for the National Conservatory of Music made Dvořák's American symphony possible, we explored how schools can develop and maintain a shared commitment to ML student success. Despite the fact that rural educators play pivotal and multifaceted roles in the education of all students, no single person can invoke a "shared vision." It takes teams of committed educators, partners, staff, and leaders to build that vision and draw upon each other's strengths to implement equitable education for rural ML students and their families.

In Chapter 4, the Third Movement comes to life. This chapter shapes a rural school's work with ML families, arguing for a fundamental recentering of how schools engage with them. Rather than viewing ML families as recipients of school services or as repositories of information, we explored how to center families using subaltern, lesser-known concepts derived from Indigenous and minoritized knowledges, such as *consejos*, *tequío*, and transcolonizing. These concepts position ML families as holders of essential knowledge and partners in educational transformation. How we invite ML families into districts, schools, and classrooms, using languages and cultural knowledge that welcome and uplift them, is critical in ensuring that MLs are valued. This chapter seeks to inspire educators to place ML families' identities and knowledge at the center of engagement practices, opening linguistic spaces for them to participate in nontraditional ways.

Finally, the Fourth Movement is illuminated in Chapter 5. This chapter addressed various forms of team-based collaboration—both within schools and across community partnerships. I discussed teacher collaboration, which is increasingly important in ML education and in rural spaces where ESL and bilingual resources are limited. Other collaborations involve school-community partnerships and university relationships. Like a symphony orchestra in which every musician must listen to and respond to others, effective rural ML education requires intentional, sustained collaboration grounded in relational trust and distributed expertise.

This final chapter brings these movements together. An Action Plan template is provided for educators, school leaders, and district teams to assess their current practices for rural MLs and to develop concrete steps to transform education for rural MLs. The Action Plan is organized around the four movements presented in Chapters 2–5, each section containing two parts:

- **Part I: Reflection and Resources**—A self-assessment of existing strengths and areas for growth in schools and classrooms
- **Part II: What We Can Do**—Action steps and strategies for implementation

This Action Plan is designed to be completed collaboratively by teams of educators. It can include not only teachers who work directly with MLs but also language specialists such as ESL teachers, administrators, bilingual paraeducators, counselors, and family liaison staff. I encourage you to adapt these templates to your specific rural context, resources, and community needs. This is essential because each rural community has a unique history, way of functioning, and relationship to the land as a place-conscious community.

How to Use This Action Plan

Before beginning, consider forming an ML team that includes diverse stakeholders from your school and community. In one small grade 3–5 elementary school where I worked, this involved the school counselor, who was responsible for conveying achievement data to ML families during parent-teacher meetings, which were held twice each year. It also included the school principal and three classroom teachers, one of whom had strong ties to the ML families through her church and her children's sports teams. Other team members might include community partners such as social service providers and even ML students themselves. The team should meet regularly to work through each section of the Action Plan, discuss findings, and develop implementation strategies. Include your bilingual paraeducators, who research shows (Oudghiri, 2023; Reeves, 2023) feel undervalued in rural settings but who have deep insider knowledge and experiences with MLs. The composition of your team matters—aim to include voices that may be marginalized in school decision-making.

Suggested Process:

1. Gather your team and review the relevant chapter from this book before addressing each section
2. Complete Part A reflection questions, assess your current practices, and identify gaps
3. Develop action steps in Part B, assigning responsibilities and timelines
4. Schedule regular check-ins to monitor progress and adjust strategies as needed

Remember that meaningful change takes time. One or two priorities from each section can make a significant difference for MLs and families. Keep the well-being and success of your rural ML students and families at the center of your work. Get to know them, their histories, their languages, and cultures.

The First Movement: Representation and Belonging

Representation and belonging form the foundation of equitable education for rural ML. When ML students see their languages, cultures, and identities reflected throughout the school environment—in the air, in the halls, and on the walls—they develop a stronger sense of belonging that supports their academic achievement and social-emotional well-being. This section guides your examination of how effectively your school creates spaces in which ML students feel seen, valued, and included. Representation is not a one-and-done event—it is an ongoing, evolving commitment that must move beyond surface-level recognition. While multicultural events such as Hispanic Heritage Month or Black History Month can serve as affirming spaces, true representation requires integrating diverse histories, languages, and cultural narratives into the fabric of education year-round (Sleeter & Grant, 2008). This means embedding multilingual practices throughout daily instruction, communication, and school life.

The concept of translanguaging—using students' full linguistic repertoires as resources for learning—is central to meaningful representation and provides the linguistic foundation for ML students to acquire a high level of English language and literacy (García & Li, 2014). When MLs are encouraged to draw on all their language skills, rather than being limited to English, they can demonstrate their knowledge and capabilities. Translanguaging affirms students' identities and positions their multilingualism as the superpower it is.

Similarly, research on sense of belonging consistently shows that students who feel accepted, valued, and included by teachers and peers perform better academically and demonstrate stronger social-emotional well-being. For ML students from diverse or vulnerable backgrounds, belonging operates as a protective factor that can shield them from the negative effects of adversity. Your work in this area has the potential to change ML students' lives.

Part I: Reflection and Resources

Use these questions to guide individual reflection and team discussion about representation and belonging in your school and classrooms.

School Environment

1. When you walk through the front entrance of your school, what languages are visible? Do they reflect the linguistic diversity of your student population?
2. What images, photographs, and artwork are displayed in hallways and common areas? Do they represent the cultural and ethnic backgrounds of your ML students and families?
3. Is important school information (calendars, announcements, safety procedures) available in the home languages of your families?
4. How does your school's marquee, website, and social media presence reflect linguistic diversity?

Classroom Practices

1. How do teachers acknowledge and incorporate students' home languages in daily instruction?
2. Are classroom libraries stocked with bilingual books and texts that reflect ML students' backgrounds? And the history of the community that includes people from diverse backgrounds?
3. Do instructional materials and curriculum include diverse perspectives and culturally relevant content?
4. How are translanguaging practices supported and encouraged in classrooms?

Sense of Belonging

1. How do ML students describe their sense of belonging at school? Have you asked them?
2. What opportunities exist for ML students to share their languages, cultures, and experiences with peers? With educators? With the community?
3. How does your school celebrate linguistic and cultural diversity beyond isolated heritage month events?
4. Are there adult role models in the school who share ML students' linguistic and cultural backgrounds?

Rural Resources

This self-assessment is to identify your school's current strengths and areas for growth related to representation and belonging (Table 6.1).

Part II: What We Can Do

Based on your reflection and resource self-assessment, identify specific steps you can take as a team to strengthen representation and belonging for your rural ML students. Consider the

TABLE 6.1 Practices for Sense of Belonging and Representation

Suggested Practices	*Status*
School signage includes the languages of ML families	☐ Yes ☐ Partial ☐ No
Visual displays reflect the cultural and linguistic diversity of students	☐ Yes ☐ Partial ☐ No
Important documents translated into MLs' home languages. Oral languages are used with nonprint literate families	☐ Yes ☐ Partial ☐ No
Classroom libraries include bilingual/multicultural books	☐ Yes ☐ Partial ☐ No
Teachers use translanguaging and first-language learning strategies in instruction	☐ Yes ☐ Partial ☐ No
Bilingual staff represent ML student backgrounds	☐ Yes ☐ Partial ☐ No
ML students report feeling welcomed and valued	☐ Yes ☐ Partial ☐ No
Students' cultural backgrounds are integrated throughout the year	☐ Yes ☐ Partial ☐ No

TABLE 6.2 Action Steps for Belonging and Representation

Action Step	*Person(s) Responsible*	*Target Date*
1.		
2.		
3.		

immediate action steps you can take within a month, short-term goals that you can meet within a semester, and long-term vision and goals for the year and beyond.

Suggested Strategies for Belonging and Representation:

- Conduct a linguistic landscape walkthrough of your school with your team
- Create multilingual welcome signs and hallway displays
- Develop a system for translating essential communications
- Audit classroom libraries for bilingual and multicultural texts
- Survey ML students about their sense of belonging
- Identify and recruit bilingual community members as volunteers or staff
- Plan cultural events that integrate throughout the school year, not just heritage months. For instance, offer bilingual books and invite bilingual community members into the school to read with children (Table 6.2).

The Second Movement: Shared Vision

A shared vision among educators is the collective north star that keeps teams together and able to progress in the same direction toward common goals for ML students. Like Jeannette Thurber's vision for inclusive music education at the National Conservatory, a shared vision for rural ML education requires collaboration, high expectations, and systemic supports. This section helps your team develop and articulate a unified vision for your ML students' success.

Developing a shared vision is challenging because, initially, the concept can seem abstract. Engaging diverse stakeholders in meaningful dialogue about what high-quality education for ML students consists of, and then translating that vision into everyday practices, resource allocation decisions, and professional development priorities. A shared vision for rural MLs must be grounded in an asset-based orientation that views bilingualism and biculturalism as strengths to be developed rather than problems to be overcome. When this asset-based stance becomes collectively held, it influences everything from how educators speak about ML students to how the school allocates resources and structures programs.

Research on shared vision emphasizes that compelling vision is not imposed from above but co-created with those who will implement it. This means involving classroom teachers, bilingual paraeducators, ML families, and community members in the visioning process—not just administrators. When educators have a voice in shaping the vision, they are more likely to work toward its realization.

Part I: Reflection and Resources

Use these questions to examine how your school develops and maintains a shared vision for serving ML students.

Vision Development

1. Does your school have an articulated vision specifically for ML student success? If so, how was it developed, and who was involved?
2. How do educators across your school describe what success looks like for ML students? Is there consistency in these descriptions?
3. How are bilingualism and biculturalism viewed in your school—as an asset to be developed or a challenge to overcome?
4. What role do ML families and community members play in shaping your school's vision?

Vision Communication

1. How is the vision for ML education communicated to all staff, teachers, and across leadership?
2. Do all educators—not just ESL and bilingual teachers—understand their role in supporting ML students?
3. How is the vision communicated to ML families in accessible ways? In what languages?

Vision Implementation

1. How does your shared vision influence hiring decisions, resource allocation, and scheduling?
2. What professional development opportunities support educators in enacting a vision for ML students and families?
3. How can you measure progress toward the vision, and how often should it be revisited?

Complete this self-assessment to evaluate your school's **shared vision** for ML students (Table 6.3).

TABLE 6.3 Practices for Shared Vision

Suggested Practices	*Current Status*
We have an articulated vision for ML student success	☐ Yes ☐ Partial ☐ No
All staff view bilingualism as an asset	☐ Yes ☐ Partial ☐ No
Educators collaborate across content areas for MLs	☐ Yes ☐ Partial ☐ No
High expectations are held for all ML students	☐ Yes ☐ Partial ☐ No
Professional development addresses ML needs	☐ Yes ☐ Partial ☐ No
ML families help shape our educational vision	☐ Yes ☐ Partial ☐ No
Resources are allocated to support ML programs, including before and after-school programs	☐ Yes ☐ Partial ☐ No
We regularly assess progress toward ML goals	☐ Yes ☐ Partial ☐ No

TABLE 6.4 Action Steps for Shared Vision

Action Step	*Person(s) Responsible*	*Target Date*
1.		
2.		
3.		

Part II: What We Can Do

Develop action steps to create, strengthen, or implement a shared vision for your rural ML students.

Suggested Strategies for Building Shared Vision:

- Host a visioning session with diverse stakeholders using de Farber's CoLAB model
- Create ML student profiles that travel with students across grades
- Establish cross-disciplinary ML team meetings
- Develop articulation plans for ML students across grade levels and school
- Pool resources across schools in your rural district
- Create opportunities for first-language support in instruction (Table 6.4)

The Third Movement: Centering Multilingual Learner Families

As discussed throughout this book, recentering ML families in family engagement means recognizing families as holders of knowledge and cultural wealth that are essential to their children's education and well-being. Drawing on concepts like *consejos* (everyday oral teachings through sayings and stories), *tequío* (community commitment and well-being), and transcolonizing (systemic transformation that includes diverse knowledges), this section helps you examine how your school positions and engages ML families—not as passive recipients of school information, but as active partners and contributors.

As we explored in Chapter 4, there is an important distinction between family involvement and family engagement. Involvement places responsibility on families to participate in school-defined activities, often at times and in ways that may not be accessible to ML families who work in distant locations and at nontraditional hours. Engagement, in contrast, is a two-way relationship built on mutual respect and shared responsibility for ML students' learning.

Rural ML families face unique barriers to engagement: long distances to school, work schedules that conflict with traditional school events, limited transportation, and—for some—concerns about immigration status that make any interaction with institutions feel unsafe. Effective family engagement in rural contexts must acknowledge and address these barriers while building on the considerable strengths of rural ML families.

The concept of funds of knowledge underscores that ML families—regardless of formal education or English proficiency—possess valuable knowledge and skills that can enrich their children's learning. When educators take time to learn about families' occupational expertise, cultural traditions, migration stories, and ways of knowing, they can draw on these funds of knowledge to make instruction more relevant and effective.

Dvořák's memories of his rural childhood—rich with music, family, labor, and community—remind us that creativity and learning flourish in economically modest and physically demanding environments. Your ML families bring a similar wealth of experience that, when recognized and honored, can transform educational practice.

Part I: Reflection and Resources

Use these questions to examine your school's approach to engaging ML families.

Family-School Relationships

1. How would you describe the current relationship between your school and ML families—is it one of partnership, providing services, or something else?

2. When you think about ML family engagement, do you focus on what families should do for the school, or what the school can learn from families?
3. How do educators in your school view ML families' knowledge and expertise? Is it valued and utilized?
4. What barriers exist for ML family participation, and how have you addressed them?
5. How are ML families' cultures, languages, vision, and voices incorporated into engagement events?

Communication and Access

1. How and when do you communicate with ML families? In what languages? In print or orally? By telephone or in writing?
2. Is interpretation always available for family-teacher conferences and school events?
3. Do you proactively reach out to ML families, or primarily wait for them to initiate contact?

Funds of Knowledge (from Moll et al., 1992)

1. What do you know about the occupational skills, cultural knowledge, and life experiences of your ML families?
2. What do you know about how ML families support one another?
3. (How) have you incorporated families' funds of knowledge into classroom instruction or school programming?
4. Do ML families have meaningful opportunities to contribute to school decision-making?

This self-assessment can help you evaluate your current **ML family engagement** practices (Table 6.5).

Develop action steps to recenter ML families in your engagement practices.

TABLE 6.5 Practices for ML Family Engagement

Suggested Practices	*Current Status*
ML families are viewed as partners with expertise	☐ Yes ☐ Partial ☐ No
Communication is accessible (language, timing, method)	☐ Yes ☐ Partial ☐ No
Interpretation is available for all school events	☐ Yes ☐ Partial ☐ No
Events are scheduled at times accessible to ML families	☐ Yes ☐ Partial ☐ No
We know and utilize ML families' funds of knowledge	☐ Yes ☐ Partial ☐ No
ML families participate in school decision-making	☐ Yes ☐ Partial ☐ No
Home visits or community outreach occur in culturally appropriate ways	☐ Yes ☐ Partial ☐ No
Wraparound services address ML family needs	☐ Yes ☐ Partial ☐ No

Part II: What We Can Do

Suggested Strategies for Centering Families:

- Conduct home visits to learn about families' strengths and needs
- Create a parent advisory committee with ML family representation *or* a unique ML family advisory committee
- Develop bilingual fotonovelas or visual guides for school processes *or* use or adapt existing fotonovelas like those provided
- Invite family members to share their expertise in classrooms
- Hold events at community locations familiar to ML families
- Partner with community organizations that serve ML families
- Recognize and value bilingual paraeducators as family liaisons

Develop action steps for **centering ML families** (Table 6.6).

TABLE 6.6 Action Steps for ML Family Engagement

Action Step	*Person(s) Responsible*	*Target Date*
1.		
2.		
3.		

The Fourth Movement: Collaboration and Community

Like a symphony orchestra where every instrument contributes to the whole, effective rural ML education requires collaboration among educators within schools and partnerships across the broader community. This final section of the Action Plan focuses on building the collaborative structures and relationships necessary to support ML students and families comprehensively. Collaboration is built on relational trust, distributed expertise, and learning from and with the community.

Rural schools face particular challenges when it comes to collaboration. Geographic isolation often leaves rural educators feeling alone in their work, with few colleagues who share their expertise or understand their ML students' needs. Small staff sizes mean that ESL teachers may be the only specialists in their building—or may serve multiple schools across vast distances. Limited budgets in rural communities and school districts constrain opportunities for professional development and collaboration time. Yet rural communities also possess unique collaborative strengths. Rural resourcefulness, ingenuity, familism, and unity act are cultural assets for schools. In addition, rural ML families hold additional assets, including funds of knowledge networks and extended family relationships, as *familismo*, particularly within and across Latino communities. The close-knit nature of rural communities means that educators often have deep insider knowledge about how their communities function and about relationships with families and community members. Rural schools frequently serve as community hubs where people come together for events and activities. The necessity of doing more with less calls for cultivated resourcefulness and creativity among rural educators.

Effective collaboration requires relational trust—relationships characterized by mutual respect, personal regard, competence, and integrity. When educators trust one another, they can engage in honest dialogue about evidence and data, take risks with new approaches, and support each other through challenges. Building this trust takes time and intentional effort, but it is the foundation upon which all other collaborative work rests.

Distributed expertise recognizes that no single person has all the answers. In rural schools, teachers and staff often perform multifaceted roles and bring diverse skills to their work. Effective collaboration identifies and leverages this distributed expertise, ensuring that the unique knowledge of bilingual paraeducators, for example, is valued and utilized alongside that of certified teachers and administrators.

Part I: Reflection and Resources

Use these questions to examine collaboration within your school and with community partners.

Within-School Collaboration

1. How do ESL, bilingual, and content-area teachers collaborate to support ML students? Is this collaboration structured or informal?
2. What role do bilingual paraeducators play in your school, and how is their expertise recognized and utilized?
3. How is information about ML students shared across teachers and grade levels?
4. What co-teaching models, if any, are used to serve ML students?

Community Partnerships

1. What community organizations, agencies, or institutions does your school partner with to support ML families?
2. How does your school connect ML families with needed services (healthcare, dental care, legal aid, social services)?
3. Are there university partnerships that support your ML programs or professional development?

Relational Trust

1. How would you characterize the level of trust among educators at your school when discussing the needs of ML students?
2. Do educators feel comfortable taking risks and trying new approaches to support ML students?
3. How do you build and maintain trust with ML families and community partners?

Complete this self-assessment to evaluate your **collaborative practices** (Table 6.7).

Part II: What We Can Do

Suggested Strategies for Collaboration:

- Implement co-teaching models (one teach/one assist, station teaching, team teaching)
- Create a scheduled collaboration time for ESL and content teachers
- Form or join a virtual community of practice for rural ML educators

TABLE 6.7 Practices for Collaboration

Practice Area	*Current Status*
ESL, bilingual, and content teachers have structured collaboration time	☐ Yes ☐ Partial ☐ No
Co-teaching models are used to serve ML students	☐ Yes ☐ Partial ☐ No
Bilingual paraeducators and family liaison staff expertise is valued and used	☐ Yes ☐ Partial ☐ No
ML student information is shared across educators	☐ Yes ☐ Partial ☐ No
Community partnerships support ML families	☐ Yes ☐ Partial ☐ No
University partnerships enhance ML programs and supports	☐ Yes ☐ Partial ☐ No
Virtual communities of practice connect rural educators	☐ Yes ☐ Partial ☐ No
High relational trust exists among staff	☐ Yes ☐ Partial ☐ No

TABLE 6.8 Action Steps for Collaboration

Action Step	*Person(s) Responsible*	*Target Date*
1.		
2.		
3.		

- Establish partnerships with local churches, community centers, and service organizations
- Connect with university teacher education programs for student teachers and interns
- Identify community connectors who can bridge school and ML families
- Pool resources across schools in your rural district

Develop action steps to strengthen **collaboration** for your rural ML students (Table 6.8).

Bringing the Four Principles Together

You have now worked through reflection questions, self-assessments, and action planning for each of the four educational movements: Representation and Belonging, Shared Vision, Recentering Families, and Team Collaboration. Like the movements of a symphony, these principles work together to create a comprehensive approach to serving rural ML students and families. As you move forward with implementation, keep the following ideas in mind.

Start Where You Are

Each rural school and district is different. Your rural context—including your community's history, resources, demographics, and relationships—shapes how you implement these principles. Build on existing strengths and address the most pressing needs first. Consider what makes your rural community unique: the industries that sustain your economy, the histories that have shaped your region, the background languages, cultures, and stories of the people, and the relationships that bind families and neighbors together. These elements of your *terroir*—your sense of place—should inform every aspect of your Action Plan.

Take time to understand the specific assets and challenges of your community. As noted earlier, rural communities possess rural cultural wealth: resourcefulness born of necessity, strong kin-like networks, community unity, and deep connections to place. These strengths can be leveraged to support ML students and families in ways that urban or suburban approaches cannot replicate. Meaningful change takes time. Set realistic goals, celebrate incremental progress, and be patient with yourselves and your colleagues. It is better to implement a few strategies well than to attempt too many changes at once. Remember that the four movements presented in this book are interconnected—progress in one area often supports growth in others—but you can equally start with assessing collaboration and then move to recentering ML families in engagement.

Include ML students and families. Their perspectives should guide your decisions and help you evaluate your progress. Too often, well-intentioned educators make decisions about ML students without consulting the students themselves or their families. This approach, however well-meaning, can perpetuate the very inequities we seek to address. Consider creating regular opportunities for ML students to share their experiences through student focus groups, informal conversations, or written reflections. Ask questions like: Do you feel welcomed at school? Can you use your home language here? Do you see yourself in what we teach and display? What would make school better for you?

Similarly, create authentic opportunities for ML families to provide input—not just at formal meetings, but through home visits, community gatherings, and ongoing dialogue. Remember that families may be more comfortable sharing in their home language, in familiar community spaces, or with bilingual staff members they have come to trust.

Build Relational Trust

The pivotal characteristic that ties these four movements together is the relationship we have with one another and with those around us. All four movements depend on strong relationships—among educators, between schools and ML families, and with various community partners. Invest time in building trust, which grows through consistent, respectful interactions. In my work in rural communities, I have a few non-negotiables. First, I always travel to and work with educators. I don't assume that rural educators will always be available when I am. Instead, I work around their constraints, such as time and geography. I travel there as frequently as possible. Second, I never go empty-handed because I respect that rural educators always give me their time, insights, and expertise. I bring supplies, food, university swag, and non-material items, such as invitations to events and professional opportunities, including conferences. Finally, I show up when I am supposed to as a way to build a consistent relationship and trust. I want rural educators to know that they can trust our relationships. As Bryk and Schneider remind us, relational trust is the connective tissue that unites educators, families, and communities around a shared commitment to children. These three non-negotiables are some of the ways that I build relational trust.

Other trust-building strategies include:

- Following through on commitments, even small ones
- Learn ML families' languages and their cultural backgrounds. Even a few words of recognition can demonstrate your desire to communicate with them
- Acknowledging mistakes and demonstrating willingness to learn
- Listening more than speaking, especially when working with families
- Sharing decision-making power with families and community members
- Being present at community events, not just school events, especially if you reside in your rural community

Learn and Advocate

Approaching this work with rural educators requires a genuine learning stance. Educators are encouraged to try new strategies, thoughtfully reflect on what is effective and what is not, and continuously adjust their practice. I have worked with bilingual educators in rural schools who realized only after participating in a professional learning community focused on ML students that their bilingualism was an asset. That moment of personal and professional realization impacted other educators in the PLC, who began to recognize the linguistic resources hidden deeply in their rural community. Creating opportunities for educators to learn from one another and from the ML families they serve is essential. Some of the most meaningful and rewarding work often occurs when educators have the time and space to collaborate in rich and meaningful ways.

While much of this Action Plan emphasizes what educators can do within their immediate contexts, it is equally important to acknowledge that supporting ML in rural schools also demands systemic change. Rural schools continue to face underfunding, and programs serving ML often face even greater resource constraints. This is particularly true in the current context of federal funding cuts and the move to eliminate safeguards previously provided by the U.S. Department of Education (Coady, 2025; Lieberman, 2025). As educators move forward with their action plans, they should also consider how to advocate for the policies and resources necessary to fully support their multilingual students.

Advocacy can take many forms. Educators might begin by documenting the needs of their multilingual learner populations and sharing this information with district and state leaders. Building connections with statewide organizations that support ML and rural education, such as state affiliates of the National Association for Bilingual Education (NABE) or TESOL International, can strengthen these efforts. Inviting policymakers to visit schools and engage directly with multilingual students and their families can also foster understanding and support. Finally, sharing success stories that highlight the positive impact of well-resourced multilingual learner programs can help demonstrate why sustained investment and advocacy truly matter.

Conclusion

This chapter presents a summary Action Plan of the ideas presented in this book, based on four key principles or movements for rural ML education: sense of belonging and representation, shared vision, recentering ML families in engagement, and collaboration and partnerships. This chapter suggests reflection spaces for educators to use collaboratively. This work must be tailored to the needs of your local community, your community and school's strengths and assets, and the resources available in your area. Place-based approaches and solutions for rural MLs are grounded in the cultural wealth of local rural communities. Together, as educators, we can reverse deficit-based practices and ideologies and create a symphony of support for rural multilingual learners, with every teacher, leader, staff member, and community partner playing an essential role in helping ML students thrive.

References

Aleaziz, H. (2025, July). Illegal border crossings plunge to lowest level in decades. *The New York Times*. https://www.nytimes.com/2025/07/02/us/politics/border-crossings-trump.html

Allen, C. J. (1988). *The hold life has: Coca and cultural identity in an Andean community*. Smithsonian Institution Press.

Arias, M. B., & Morillo-Campbell, M. (2008). *Promoting ELL parental involvement: Challenges in contested times*. Education Policy Research Unit. https://epsl.asu.edu/epru/documents/EPSL-0801-250-EPRU.pdf

August, D., & Shanahan, T. (Eds.). (2006). *Developing literacy in second-language learners: Report of the National Literacy Panel on Language-Minority Children and Youth*. Lawrence Erlbaum Associates Publishers.

Azano, A. (2011). The possibility of place: One teacher's use of place-based instruction for English students in a rural high school. *Journal of Research in Rural Education, 26*(10). https://jrre.psu.edu/articles/26-10.pdf

Azano, A., Flowers, J., Coady, M. R., & Biddle, C. (2025). Trends influencing the future of rural education research in the United States. In H. Harmon & J. Johnson (Eds.), *Handbook on rural and remote education*. Elgar.

Azano, A. P., & Stewart, T. T. (2016). Confronting challenges at the intersection of rurality, place, and teacher preparation: Improving efforts in teacher education to staff rural schools. *Global Education Review, 3*(1), 108–128.

Banther, J., & Bukowski, B. (2021, February). Dvořák's symphony No. 9: "From the New World." The origins and inspirations you didn't know. *Classical Breakdown*. https://weta.org/fm/features/classical-breakdown/Dvořáks-symphony-no-9-new-world-origins-and-inspirations-you-didnt

Banther, J., & Keely, E. (2024, February). The life and music of Antonin Dvořák: From humble beginnings to stardom! *Classical Breakdown*. https://weta.org/fm/features/classical-breakdown/life-and-music-antonin-Dvořák-humble-beginnings-stardom

Baquedano-López, P., Hernández, S., & Alexander, R. (2014). Thinking through the decolonial turn in research and praxis. In P. R. Portes et al. (Eds.), *U.S. Latinos and education policy: Research-based directions for change*. Routledge.

Barnett, K., & McCormick, J. (2003). Vision, relationships and teacher motivation: A case study. *Journal of Educational Administration, 41*(1), 55–73.

Beckerman, M. (2003). *New worlds of Dvořák: Searching in America for the composer's inner life*. Norton.

Bennett, K. J., Borders, T. F., Holmes, G. M., Kozhimannil, K. B., & Ziller, E. (2019). What is rural? Challenges and implications of definitions that inadequately encompass rural people and places. *Health Affairs, 38*(12), 1985–1992.

Bialystok, E. (2011). Reshaping the mind: The benefits of bilingualism. *Canadian Journal of Experimental Psychology, 65*(4), 229–235. https://doi.org/10.1037/a0025406

Bialystok, E. (2021). Cognitive effects of bilingualism: An evolving perspective. In W. S. Francis (Ed.), *Bilingualism across the lifespan* (pp. 9–28). Routledge. https://doi.org/10.4324/9781315143996-3

Brenner, D., Azano, A. P., & Downey, J. (2021). Helping new teachers stay and thrive in rural schools. *Phi Delta Kappan, 103*(4), 14–18. https://doi.org/10.1177/00317217211065821

Bryk, A. S., & Schneider, B. (2002). *Trust in schools: A core resource for improvement*. Russell Sage Foundation.

Bryk, A. S., & Schneider, B. (2003). Trust in schools: A core resource for school reform. *Educational Leadership, 60*(6), 40–44.

Buchs, C., & Maradan, O. (2021). Fostering equity in a multicultural and multilingual classroom through cooperative learning. *Intercultural Education, 32*(4), 401–416.

Carrillo Carrasquillo, M. H., Amaya, A., & Coady, M. R. (2026, forthcoming). When monolingual frameworks fail: Border thinking and linguistic identity in rural schools. In E. McHenry-Sorber & S. Hartman (Eds.), *Critical theory in rural education: Power, place, and justice*. Routledge.

Castañeda v. Pickard, 648 F.2d 989 (5th Cir. 1981).

Ceballo, R., Maurizi, L. K., Suarez, G. A., & Aretakis, M. T. (2014). Gift and sacrifice: Parental involvement in Latino adolescents' education. *Cultural Diversity & Ethnic Minority Psychology, 20*(1), 116–127. https://doi.org/10.1037/a0033472

Coady, M. (2009). "*Solamente libros importantes*": Literacy practices and ideologies of migrant farmworking families in north central Florida. In G. Li (Ed.), *Multicultural families, home literacies and mainstream schooling* (pp. 113–128). New Age.

Coady, M. R. (2019). Rural multilingual family engagement. *The Rural Educator, 40*(3), 1–13. https://doi.org/10.35608/ruraled.v40i3.545

Coady, M. R. (2020). A review of rural English learner education: Call for a focused national research agenda. *Educational Researcher, 49*(7), 524–532. https://doi.org/10.3102/0013189X20931505

Coady, M. R. (2021). English learners in rural schools. In A. P. Azano, K. Eppley, & C. Biddle (Eds.), *The Bloomsbury handbook of rural education in the U.S.A.* (pp. 247–255). Bloomsbury.

Coady, M. R. (2025, November 12). *What the death of OELA means for rural schools–and how educators can respond*. National Rural Education Association. https://nrea.net/maria-coady-death-of-oela/

Coady, M. R., Ankeny, B., & Ankeny, R. (2022). Language as a "right": Unpacking *Castañeda*'s reach across federal, state, and district lines. *Language Policy, 21*, 305–329. https://doi.org/10.1007/s10993-021-09604-1

Coady, M. R., Coady, T. J., & Nelson, A. (2015). Assessing the needs of immigrant, Latino families and teachers in rural settings: Building home-school partnerships. *NABE Journal of Research and Practice, 6*. https://www2.nau.edu/nabej-p/ojs/index.php/njrp/article/view/42

Coady, M. R., & Escamilla, K. (2005). Audible voices, visible tongues: Exploring social realities in Spanish-speaking students' writing. *Language Arts, 82*(6), 462–471. https://www.jstor.org/stable/41483515?seq=1#page_scan_tab_contents

Coady, M. R., Golombek, P., & Marichal, N. (Eds.). (2023a). *Educating multilingual learners in rural schools: Illuminating diversity in rural communities in the United States*. Series Editor W. Reynolds. Brill.

Coady, M. R., Harper, C. A., & de Jong, E. J. (2011). Preservice to practice: Mainstream elementary teacher beliefs of preparation and efficacy with English language learners in the state of Florida. *Bilingual Research Journal, 34*(2), 223–239.

Coady, M. R., Koch, J., Carrillo, M. H., Dali, Z., López Caicedo, R., Rubinstein, C., & Amaya, A. (2026, April). *Reimagining place as a critical theory tenet in rural dual language immersion programs* [Conference presentation]. *American Educational Research Association Annual Meeting*, Los Angeles, CA, United States.

Coady, M. R., Lewis, B., & Mann, J. (2024). "Send me a picture and I'll tell you what it says": Language as rural cultural wealth in rural multilingual family engagement. *Journal of Education and Multilingualism, 1*(2), 190–224. https://jempub.com/wp-content/uploads/2024/12/Coady_Et_Al_2024_Send_Me_A.pdf

Coady, M. R., Marichal, N., Olszewska, A., Ankeny, R., Long, A., Shafiei, H., & Chakraborty, R. (2023b). "It's like fuel": Igniting rural English learner education through place-conscious professional development. *Journal of Research in Rural Education, 39*(1). https://doi.org/10.26209/JRRE3901

Coady, M. R., Miller, D., Zeyjun, J., Heffington, D. V., Lopez, M. P. S., Olszewska, A., de Jong, E. J., Yilmaz, T., & Ankeny, R. (2020). Can effective teaching be observed? Validation of an EL-modified Framework for Teaching observation protocol. *TESOL Quarterly, 54*(1), 173–200. https://doi.org/10.1002/tesq.544

Coady, M. R., & Moore, C. (2010). Using *Libros*: The emergent bi-literacy development of Spanish-speaking children. *TESOL Journal, 2*, 91–108.

Coady, M. R., & Roberson, J. L. (2024). The shifting linguistic landscape on Ocracoke Island. In J. Reaser, W. Wolfram & C. Gaskill (Eds.), *Language and Life on Ocracoke: The Living History of the Brogue* (pp. 235–242). UNC Press.

Coady, M. R., & Román, D. (2024). Introduction to the special topics issue on rural multilingual education. *The Rural Educator, 45*(4), i–v. https://doi.org/10.55533/2643-9662.1542

Coady, M. R. & Sorel, T. (2019). *Small Town, Big Dreams*. https://www.youtube.com/watch?v=qP4sbLce5sM

Coleman, J. S. (1988). Social capital in the creation of human capital. *American Journal of Sociology, 94*, S95–S120.

Collier, V. P., & Thomas, W. P. (2017). Validating the power of bilingual schooling: Thirty-two years of large-scale, longitudinal research. *Annual Review of Applied Linguistics, 37*, 203–217.

Corbett, M. (2020). Place-based education: A critical appraisal from a rural perspective. In M. Corbett & D. Gereluk (Eds.), *Rural teacher education* (pp. 89–108). Springer. https://doi.org/10.1007/978-981-15-2560-5_14

Cranley, E., Román, D., Wilfred, J., Coady, M. R., & Amaya, A. (2025). *Illuminating place and rurality in multilingual and dual language education*. WIDA Spotlight Session.

Crumb, L., Chambers, C., Azano, A., Cuthrell, K., & Avent, M. (2022). Rural cultural wealth: Dismantling deficit ideologies of rurality. *Journal for Multicultural Education*. https://doi.org/10.1108/JME-06-2022-0076

Cummins, J. (2000). *Language, power, and pedagogy: Bilingual children in the crossfire*. Multilingual Matters.

de Farber, B. G. (2021). *Creating fundable grant proposals: Profiles of innovative partnerships*. ALA.

de Farber, B. G., Hines, A., & Hood, B. J. (2017). *Collaborating with strangers: Facilitating workshops in libraries, classrooms, and non-profits*. ALA.

de la Luz Reyes, M. (2015). *Words were all we had: Becoming biliterate against the odds*. Teachers College Press.

Dean Hughes, M., Coady, M. R., Robeson, J., Estrada, M., & Montesinos Jorro, R. (2026, in press). "I bet I can do that": Rural cultural wealth in a grow-your-own (GYO) teacher education program. *Theory and Practice in Rural Education*.

Delgado-Gaitán, C. (1994). Consejos: The power of cultural narratives. *Anthropology & Education Quarterly*, *25*(3), 298–316. https://doi.org/10.1525/aeq.1994.25.3.04x0146p

DeNicolo, C. P. (2019). The role of translanguaging in establishing school belonging for emergent multilinguals. *International Journal of Inclusive Education*, *23*(9), 967–984.

DeNicolo, C. P., González, M., Morales, S., & Romaní, L. (2017). Teaching through testimonio: Accessing community cultural wealth in school. *Journal of Latinos and Education*, *14*(4), 228–243. https://doi.org/10.1080/15348431.2014.1000541

DeNicolo, C. P., Roberts, K. L., Brooks, R., Puente, A., & Stanczyk, A. (2024). Pedagogy and practice: Creating spaces for multilingual learners to create and belong. *Journal of Language & Literacy Education*, *20*(1), 1–17.

Deslandes, R., Royer, E., Turcotte, D. & Bertrand, R. (1997). School achievement at the secondary level: Influence of parenting style and parent involvement in schooling. *McGill Journal of Education*, *32*, 191–207. https://mje.mcgill.ca/article/view/8377

Dickson, E., Lardier, D. T., Verdezoto, C. S., & Hackett, J. M. (2024). Reducing isolation for educators through ECHO virtual communities of practice. *Frontiers in Education*, *9*, Article 1409721. https://doi.org/10.3389/feduc.2024.1409721

Discovering masterpieces of classical music: Dvořák [Film]. (2007). Films Media Group. https://fod.infobase.com/PortalPlaylists.aspx?wID=238336&xtid=59070

Dove, M. G., & Honigsfeld, A. (2018). *Co-teaching for English learners: A guide to collaborative planning, instruction, assessment, and reflection*. Corwin.

DuFour, R., DuFour, R., Eaker, R., Many, T., & Mattos, M. (2016). *Learning by doing* (3rd ed.). Solution Tree.

DuFour, R., & Eaker, R. (1998). *Professional learning communities at work*. Solution Tree.

Dvořák, A. (n.d.). *From the memories of Antonín Dvořák: Recollections of the Prague organ school* (J. Michl Retold, & R. F. Samsour, Trans.). Antonín Dvořák: The Official Website. https://www.antonin-Dvořák.cz/en/Dvořák-on-himself/from-the-memories-of-antonin-Dvořák/

Epstein, J. L. (2011). *School, family, and community partnerships: Preparing educators and improving schools* (2nd ed.). Westview Press.

Equal Educational Opportunity Act of 1974, 20 U.S.C. §§ 1701–1758 (2018).

Escamilla, K. (2022). *The science of reading for multilingual learners: What educators need to know* [Video]. Linguistic Diversity Speaker Series, North Carolina State University. https://vimeo.com/804111801

Escamilla, K., Hopewell, S., Butvilofsky, S., Sparrow, W., Soltero-González, L., Ruiz Figueroa, O., & Escamilla, M. (2014). *Biliteracy from the start: Literacy squared in action*. Caslon Publishing.

Escamilla, K., Olsen, L., & Slavick, J. (2022). *Toward comprehensive effective literacy policy and instruction for English learner/emergent bilingual students*. National Center for Effective Literacy. https://multilingualliteracy.org/wp-content/uploads/2022/04/21018-NCEL-Effective-Literacy-White-Paper-FINAL_v2.0.pdf

Flores, R. Q., Morgan, P., Rivera, L., & Clark, C. (2019). Latinx family engagement in schools and surrounding communities: Assessing the impact of parent (and other family member) development on improving student educational outcomes at Gene Ward Elementary School. *Education Sciences*, *9*(2), 149.

Fradette, R. (2019, November 26). They see themselves in her: Immokalee Community School principal finds her voice. *Naple News*. https://www.naplesnews.com/story/news/education/2019/11/26/immokalee-community-school-principal-comes-home/4157885002/

Freire, P. (1970). *Pedagogy of the oppressed*. Continuum.

Gagnon, D. (2020, April 1). *Strengthening English learner education in rural areas*. Institute of Education Sciences Blog. https://ies.ed.gov/learn/blog/strengthening-english-learner-education-rural-areas

García, O. (2024). *Translanguaging: Equity for bilingual learners* [Video]. Linguistic Diversity Speaker Series, North Carolina State University. https://www.youtube.com/watch?v=JHxeCZqTAIk

García, O., & Kleifgen, J. A., & Cervantes-Soon, C. (2025). *Educating emergent bilinguals: Policies, programs, and practices for English learners* (3rd ed.). Teachers College Press.

García, O., & Kleyn, T. (2016). *Translanguaging with multilingual students: Learning from classroom moments*. Routledge.

García, O., & Li, W. (2014). *Translanguaging: Language, bilingualism and education*. Palgrave Macmillan.

Gardot, M. (2021). *Moon River* [Video]. Le Grand Studio RTL. https://www.youtube.com/watch?v=qQVA4QSU-fM

Golombek, P., Olszewska, A., & Coady, M. R. (2022). The humanizing power of counter-stories: Teachers' understandings of emerging bilinguals in rural settings. *Teaching and Teacher Education*, (113), 1–21. https://doi.org/10.1016/j.tate.2022.103655

Goodall, J., & Montgomery, C. (2014). Parental involvement to parental engagement: A continuum. *Educational Review*, *66*(4), 399–410. https://doi.org/10.1080/00131911.2013.781576

Goodenow, C. (1993). The psychological sense of school membership among adolescents: Scale development and educational correlates. *Psychology in the Schools*, *30*(1), 79–90.

Gorter, D. (2006). Introduction: The study of the linguistic landscape as a new approach to multilingualism. *International Journal of Multilingualism*, *3*(1), 1–6.

Gorter, D. (2018). Linguistic landscapes and trends in the study of schoolscapes. *Linguistics and Education*, *44*, 80–85.

Gray, D. L., Hope, E. C., & Matthews, J. S. (2018). Black and belonging at school: A case for interpersonal, instructional, and institutional opportunity structures. *Educational Psychologist*, *53*(2), 97–113.

Greenwood, D. (2019). Place, land, and the decolonization of the settler soul. *The Journal of Environmental Education*, *50*(4-6), 358–377.

Greiman, L., Leopold, A., Ipsen, C., & Myers, A. (2023). Mapping the digital divide: What predicts internet access across America? *Local Development & Society*, *6*(1), 30–42. https://doi.org/10.1080/26883597.2023.2229962

Griffith, J. (2023). Rural roulette: The battle for school vouchers and the inequitable effect on rural Texas schools. *Texas Tech Law Review*, *56*, 845.

Gruenewald, D. A. (2003). The best of both worlds: A critical pedagogy of place. *Educational Researcher, 32*(4), 3–12.

Hamman, L., Beck, E. & Donaldson, A. (2018). A pedagogy of translanguaging. *Language Magazine.* https://languagemagazine.com/2018/09/10/a-pedagogy-of-translanguaging/

Hamman-Ortiz, L. (2024). Cultivating a critical translanguaging space in dual language bilingual education, *International Multilingual Research Journal, 18*(2), 119–139. https://doi.org/10.1080/19313152.2023.2277101

Hargreaves, A. (2007). Sustainable professional learning communities. In L. Stoll, & K. S. Louis (Eds.), *Professional Learning Communities: Divergence, Depth and Dilemmas* (pp. 181–195), McGraw-Hill Education.

Harklau, L. (2000). From the "good kids" to the "worst": Representations of English language learners across educational settings. *TESOL Quarterly, 34*(1), 35–67.

Harris, A., & Jones, M. (2010). Professional learning communities and system improvement. *School Effectiveness and School Improvement, 21*(1), 1–2.

He, B., & Thompson, C. (2022). Family involvement and English learners' outcomes: A synthetic analysis. *International Review of Education, 68*(3), 409–440. https://doi.org/10.1007/s11159-022-09958-6

Henderson, A. T. & Mapp, K. L. (2002). *A new wave of evidence: School, family, and community connections on student achievement.* National Center for Family & Community Schools. Southeast Educational Development Laboratory.

Hepburn, A. (1961). *Moon River* [Song performed in film]. In *Breakfast at Tiffany's.* Paramount Pictures. https://www.youtube.com/watch?v=uirBWk-qd9A

Hord, S. M. (1997). *Professional learning communities: Communities of continuous inquiry and improvement.* Southwest Educational Development Laboratory.

Howley, C., & Howley, A. (2014). Making sense of rural education research: Art, transgression, and other acts of terroir. In S. White & M. Corbett (Eds.), *Doing educational research in rural settings: Methodological issues, international perspectives, and practical solutions* (pp. 7–25). Routledge.

Huffman, J. B. (2003). The role of shared values and vision in creating professional learning communities. *NASSP Bulletin, 87*(637), 21–34.

Ishimaru, A. (2013). From heroes to organizers. Principals and education organizing in urban school reform. *Educational Administration Quarterly*, *49*(1), 3–51. https://doi.org/10.1177/0013161X12448250

Jasis, P. M., & Ordoñez-Jasis, R. (2012). Latino parent involvement: Examining commitment and empowerment in schools. *Urban Education*, *47*(1), 65–89. https://doi.org/10.1177/0042085911416013

Jeynes, W. H. (2003). A meta-analysis: The effects of parental involvement on minority children's academic achievement. *Education and Urban Society*, *35(*2), 202–218.

Jeynes, W. H. (2017). A meta-analysis: The relationship between parental involvement and Latino student outcomes. *Education and Urban Society*, *49*(1), 4–28. https://doi.org/10.1177/0013124516630596

John, K. D., & Ford, D. R. (2017). The rural is nowhere: Bringing indigeneity and urbanism into educational research. In W. M. Reynolds (Ed.), *Forgotten places: Critical studies in rural education* (pp. 3–14). Peter Lang.

Kose, B. W. (2011). Developing a transformative school vision. *Educational Administration Quarterly*, *47*(3), 394–425.

Kouzes, J. M., & Posner, B. Z. (2008). *The leadership challenge* (4th ed.). Jossey-Bass.

Kurland, H., Peretz, H., & Hertz-Lazarowitz, R. (2010). Leadership style and organizational learning. *The Learning Organization*, *17*(2), 146–162.

Landsman, J., & Lewis, C. W. (Eds.). (2023). *White teachers/diverse classrooms: Creating inclusive schools, building on students' diversity, and providing true educational equity*. Taylor & Francis Group.

Layton, R. (Ed.). (1995). *A guide to the symphony*. Oxford University Press.

Leech, N. L., Haug, C. A., Rodriguez, E., & Gold, M. (2022). Why teachers remain teaching in rural districts: Listening to the voices from the field. *The Rural Educator*, *43*(3), 1–9. https://doi.org/10.55533/2643-9662.1340

Lewis, J. (2020). *The story behind the nostalgic melody by Dvořák that became the song "Goin' Home"*. https://www.wrti.org/arts-desk/2020-11-16/the-story-behind-the-nostalgic-melody-by-dvorak-that-became-the-song-goin-home

Lewis, L., & Gray, L. (2016). *Programs and services for high school English learners in public school districts: 2015–16* (NCES 2016-150). U.S. Department of Education, National Center for Education Statistics.

Li, S. (2020). *Ethics and Emotions of Teacher Identity in Teaching English Language Learners for Mainstream Elementary Teachers in Rural Florida*. Unpublished doctoral dissertation. University of Florida.

Lichter, D.T., & Johnson, K. M. (2020). A demographic lifeline? Immigration and Hispanic population growth in rural America. *Population Research and Policy Review*, *39*, 785–803.

Lichter, D. T., Parisi, D., & Taquino, M. C. (2018). White integration or segregation? The racial and ethnic transformation of rural and small town America. *City & Community*, *17*(3), 702–719.

Lieberman, M. (2025, June 25). How rural schools are faring under Trump. *Education Week*. https://www.edweek.org/leadership/how-rural-schools-are-faring-under-trump/2025/06

Longfellow, H. W. (1855). *The song of Hiawatha*. https://www.hwlongfellow.org/poems_poem.php?pid=296

López, F., Rivas-Drake, D., Serrano, E., & Delcid, G. (2025). The role of asset-based pedagogy in promoting belonging and ethnic-racial identity among Latine students. *Educational Psychology Review*, *37*(1), 16. https://doi.org/10.1007/s10648-025-09992-4

Lucas, T., & Villegas, A. M. (2013). Preparing linguistically responsive teachers: Laying the foundation in preservice teacher education. *Theory Into Practice*, *52*(2), 98–109. https://doi.org/10.1080/00405841.2013.770327

Luxemburg-Casco Schools. (2024). Project RESPECT. https://doorcountypulse.com/project-respect-at-luxemburg-casco-school/

Mannheim, B. (1986). The language of reciprocity in southern Peruvian Quechua. *Anthropological Linguistics*, *28*(3), 267–273.

Marichal, N., Rosario Roldán, A., & Coady, M. (2021). "My language learners seemed like ghosts": A rural teacher's transformational journey implementing the Seal of Biliteracy. Promising practices. *The Rural Educator*, *42*(1), 52–56.

Martínez-Cortés, J., & Romo, H. (2025). First-generation Latina college students' reflections of Mexican immigrant parent engagement in their college-going experiences. *Association of Mexican American Educators Journal*, *18*(1), 1–30. https://doi.org/10.24974/amae.18.1.508

Matthews, J. S., Boomhower, K. M., & Ekwueme, C. (2024). Assimilationist, reformist, and sociopolitical phases of school belonging research: A critical race and optimal distinctiveness review. In *Advances in Motivation Science* (Vol. 11, pp. 171–213). Elsevier.

McField, G. P., & McField, D. R. (2014). The consistent outcome of bilingual education programs: A meta-analysis of meta-analyses. In G. P. McField (Ed.), *The miseducation of English learners* (pp. 267–298). Information Age.

McInerney, K. (2023). Perceptions from newcomer multilingual adolescents: Predictors and experiences of sense of belonging in high school. *Child & Youth Care Forum*, *52*, 1041–1072. https://doi.org/10.1007/s10566-022-09723-8

Menken, K. & Solorza, C. (2013). Where have all the bilingual programs gone?!: Why prepared school leaders are essential for bilingual education. *Journal of Multilingual Education Research*, *4*(3). https://fordham.bepress.com/jmer/vol4/iss1/3

Menken, K., & Solorza, C. (2015). Principals as linchpins in bilingual education: The need for prepared school leaders. *International Journal of Bilingual Education and Bilingualism*, *18*(6), 676–697.

Mitchell, C., & Sackney, L. (2006). Learning communities: Creating a culture of sustained learning. *Journal of Educational Administration*, *44*(5), 474–489.

Moffa, E., & McHenry-Sorber, E. (2018). Learning to be rural: Lessons about being rural in teacher education programs. *The Rural Educator*, *39*(1), 26–40.

Moll, L. C., Amanti, C., Neff, D., & González, N. (1992). Funds of knowledge for teaching: Using a qualitative approach to connect homes and classrooms. *Theory Into Practice*, *31*(2), 132–141.

Morales-Alexander, Y. (2021). "School is the child's second home": Family engagement from a Latino sociocultural perspective. *Journal of Early Childhood Teacher Education*, *42*(4), 455–473. https://doi.org/10.1080/10901027.2020.1799118

Morita-Mullaney, T. (2021). Multilingual multiliteracies of emergent bilingual families: Transforming teachers' perspectives on the "literacies" of family engagement. *Theory Into Practice*, *60*(1), 83–93. https://doi.org/10.1080/00405841.2020.1829382

Murphy, J., Smylie, M., Mayrowetz, D., & Louis, K. S. (2009). The role of the principal in fostering the development of distributed leadership. *School Leadership and Management*, *29*(2), 181–214.

Murphy, J., & Torre, D. (2014). *Creating productive cultures in schools*. Corwin.

Murphy, J., Weil, M., Hallinger, P., & Mitman, A. (1982). Academic press: Translating high expectations into school policies and classroom practices. *Educational Leadership, 40*(3), 22–26.

Najarro, I., & Harwin, A. (2025, November 24). The widespread effects of immigration enforcement on schools in charts. *Education Week*. https://www.edweek.org/leadership/the-widespread-effects-of-immigration-enforcement-on-schools-in-charts/2025/11

National Association for Family, School, and Community Engagement. (NAFSCE). (2024). Definition of family engagement. https://nafsce.org/page/definition

National Center for Education Statistics. (2007). *Status of education in rural America (NCES 2007-040)*. U.S. Department of Education. https://nces.ed.gov/pubs2007/2007040.pdf

National Center for Education Statistics. (2021a). *Digest of education statistics: Table 214.40—English-learner (EL) students, by selected district locale and state: Selected years, fall 2003 through fall 2019*. U.S. Department of Education. https://nces.ed.gov/programs/digest/d21/tables/dt21_214.40.asp

National Center for Education Statistics. (2021b). *Condition of education: English learners in rural localities*. U.S. Department of Education. https://nces.ed.gov/programs/coe/indicator/lcc/english-learners-rural

National Center for Education Statistics. (2023a). Enrollment and school choice in rural areas. In *The condition of education 2023*. U.S. Department of Education. https://nces.ed.gov/programs/coe/indicator/lcb/school-choice-rural

National Center for Education Statistics. (2023b). *Condition of education: English learner students enrolled in public schools*. U.S. Department of Education. https://nces.ed.gov/programs/coe/indicator/cgf/english-learners

National Center for Education Statistics. (2023c). *Educational experiences—Enrollment and school choice in rural areas [Locale classification system]*. U.S. Department of Education. https://nces.ed.gov/surveys/annualreports/goods/eaa-indicator_topics/pdfs/LCS_508c.pdf

National Clearinghouse for English Language Acquisition. (2023). *Dual language education programs: Current state policies and practices*. U.S. Department of Education.

Noddings, N. (2005). *The challenge to care in schools: An alternative approach to education* (2nd ed.). Teachers College Press.

North Carolina Department of Public Instruction. (2024). EL headcount. https://drive.google.com/file/d/1t8GENj90gzkkEs1maT1nQdzvnuxKUXt2/view

OECD. (2017). *PISA 2015 results (Volume III): Students' well-being*. OECD Publishing.

Olszewska, A. (2020). *Counter-stories from Poland: Identities and language identities of adolescent refugee-background student*. [Doctoral dissertation, University of Florida]. ProQuest Dissertations and Theses Global. https://www.proquest.com/openview/24494054256cd4d4a2f80de7c78b138d/1?pqorigsite=gscholar&cbl=18750&diss=y

Oudghiri, S. (2023). Centering the voices of rural immigrant paraeducators. In M. R. Coady, P. Golombek, & N. V. Marichal (Eds.), *Educating multilingual students in rural schools: Illuminating diversity in rural communities in the United States* (pp. 98–126). Brill.

Pearson, L. D. (2024, February). *Factsheet: Trump's rescission of protected areas policies undermines safety for all*. National Immigration Law Center. https://www.nilc.org/resources/factsheet-trumps-rescission-of-protected-areas-policies-undermines-safety-for-all/

Pekarsky, D. (2007). Vision and education. *Educational Theory*, *57*(1), 103–117.

Pipa, A. F., & Geismar, N. (2020). *Reimagining rural policy: Organizing federal assistance to maximize rural prosperity*. Brookings Institution.

Population Reference Bureau. (2003, July 1). *Child poverty remains high for rural and small-town America*. https://www.prb.org/resources/child-poverty-remains-high-for-rural-and-small-town-america

Porter, L., Vázquez Cano, M., & Umansky, I. (2023). *Bilingual education and America's future: Evidence and pathways*. The Civil Rights Project/Proyecto Derechos Civiles, UCLA.

Protacio, S., Piazza, S. V., David, V., & Tigchelaar, M. (2020). Elementary teachers' initiatives in engaging families of English learners. *School Community Journal*, *30*(2), 211–227.

Qin, D. B., & Wan, C. (2015). The role of school belonging in predicting educational outcomes among Asian American adolescents. *Asian American Journal of Psychology*, *6*(4), 334–344.

Reeves, J. (2023). Bilingual paraeducators' navigation of narrow identity spaces in a rural elementary school. In M. R. Coady, P. Golombek, & N. V. Marichal (Eds.), *Educating multilingual students in rural schools: Illuminating diversity in rural communities in the United States* (pp. 70–97). Brill.

Rhinesmith, E., Anglum, J. C., Park, A., & Burrola, A. (2023). Recruiting and Retaining Teachers in Rural Schools: A Systematic Review of the Literature. *Peabody Journal of Education*, *98*(4), 347–363. https://doi.org/10.1080/0161956X.2023.2238491

Roffey, S. (2013). Inclusive and exclusive belonging: The impact on individual and community wellbeing. *Educational and Child Psychology, 30*(1), 38–49.

Rubin, E. (1990). Jeannette Meyers Thurber and the National Conservatory of Music. *American Music*, *8*(3), 294–325. https://www.jstor.org/stable/3052098

Ruecker, T. (2021). ESL programs in rural high schools: Challenges and opportunities. *The Rural Educator*, *42*(3), 14–27. https://doi.org/10.35608/ruraled.v42i3.1167

Ruiz, R. (1984). Orientations in language planning. *NABE Journal*, *8*(2), 15–34.

Rural Women's Health Project. (2025). The fotonovela. https://www.rwhp.org/fotonovela.html

Schissel, J. L. (2025). Humanizing assessment: Decolonizing, historicizing, and communing with language-minoritized communities. *Critical Inquiry in Language Studies*, *22*(2), 128–145.

Senge, P. M. (1990). *The fifth discipline: The art and practice of the learning organization*. Doubleday.

Senge, P. M., Cambron-McCabe, N., Lucas, T., Smith, B., & Dutton, J. (2012). *Schools that learn: A fifth discipline fieldbook for educators, parents, and everyone who cares about education* (Revised ed.). Doubleday.

Sheppard, B., Brown, J., & Dibbon, D. (2009). School district leadership matters. *Leadership and Policy in Schools*, *8*(3), 201–219.

Shim, J. M. (2013). Involving the parents of English language learners in a rural area: Focus on the dynamics of teacher-parent interactions. *The Rural Educator*, *34*(3), 18–26. https://doi.org/10.35608/ruraled.v34i3.396

Shohamy, E. (2006). *Language policy: Hidden agendas and new approaches*. Routledge.

Shumow, L. & Miller, J. D. (2001). Parents' at-home and at-school academic involvement with young adolescents. *Journal of Early Adolescence, 21*, 68–91. https://doi.org/10.1177/0272431601021001004

Sleeter, C. E., & Grant, C. A. (2008). *Making choices for multicultural education: Five approaches to race, class, and gender* (6th ed.). Wiley.

Smaczny, J. (1995). The Czech symphony. In R. Layton (Ed.), *A guide to the symphony* (pp. 220–261). Oxford University Press.

Soto, G. (1993). *Too many tamales*. G.P. Putnam's Sons.

Sourek, O. (1954). *Antonín Dvořák Letters and Reminiscences*. Artia.

Spelorzi, R., Schnelten, E. M., Mathers, C., & Sorace, A. (2021). More than one language: Understanding the educational benefits of bilingualism. In *A transdisciplinary lens for bilingual education* (pp. 55–75). Routledge.

Stolp, S., & Smith, S. (1995). *Transforming school culture*. ERIC Clearinghouse.

Sutton, D., Kearney, A., & Ashton, K. (2021). Improving educational inclusion for refugee-background learners through appreciation of diversity. *International Journal of Inclusive Education, 27*(6), 671–688.

Téllez, K., & Waxman, H. C. (2010). A review of research on effective community programs for English language learners. *School Community Journal, 20*(1), 103–119.

Thomas, W., & Collier, V. (2002). *A national study of school effectiveness for language minority students' long-term academic achievement: Final report*. Center for Research on Education, Diversity & Excellence. https://www.usc.edu/dept/education/CMMR/CollierThomasComplete.pdf

Thompson, S. C., & McKelvy, E. (2007). Shared Vision, Team Learning and Professional Learning Communities. National Middle School Association (NJ1), *Middle Ground, 10*(3), 12–14.

Todor, E. M. (2014). The hidden curriculum of schoolscapes: Overview of the bilingual school context. *Romanian Journal of Literary Studies, 4*, 529–538.

Unger, J. B., Cabassa, L. J., Molina, G. B., Contreras, S., & Baron, M. (2013). Evaluation of a fotonovela to increase depression knowledge and reduce stigma among Hispanic adults. *Journal of Immigrant and Minority Health, 15*, 398–406. https://doi.org/10.1007/s10903-012-9623-5

United States, Executive Office of the President. (2025a, January 29). *Executive Order No. 14151* (90 Fed. Reg. 8339).

United States, Executive Office of the President. (2025b, March 6). *Executive Order 14224: Designating English as the Official Language of the United States* (90 Fed. Reg. 11363).

US Department of Education. (2016). §§ 1116, 3115. *Every Student Succeeds Act of 2015*. https://www.ed.gov/essa?src=rn

US Department of Education. (2025, January). *Parent and family engagement: Title I, Part A of the Elementary and Secondary Education Act.* Non-regulatory guidance. https://www.ed.gov/media/document/parent-and-family-engagement-guidance-2025-109202.pdf

U.S. Department of Education. (2025, May). Proposed education skinny budget. https://www.ed.gov/media/document/fiscal-year-2026-budget-summary-110043.pdf

Uslu, F., & Gizir, S. (2017). School belonging of adolescents: The role of teacher–student relationships, peer relationships and family involvement. *Educational Sciences: Theory and Practice*, *17*(1), 63–82.

Vintan, A., & Gallagher, T. L. (2019). Collaboration to support ESL education: Complexities of the integrated model. *TESL Canada Journal*, *36*(2), 68–90. https://doi.org/10.18806/tesl.v36i2.1314

Walsh-Dilley, M. (2017). Theorizing reciprocity: Andean cooperation and the reproduction of community in highland Bolivia. *Journal of Latin American and Caribbean Anthropology*, *22*(3), 514–535.

Wang, C. L., & Rafiq, M. (2009). Organizational learning and innovation. *Journal of Small Business and Enterprise Development*, *16*(4), 580–599.

Wenger, E. (1998). *Communities of practice: Learning, meaning, and identity*. Cambridge University Press.

White, R. S., Schneider, J., & Mavrogordato, M. (2023). bELonging: Do students classified as English learners feel included? *AERA Open*, *9*. https://doi.org/10.1177/23328584231179171

Williams, H. P., & Ditch, R. W. (2019). Co-teaching: Equity for English learners? *Theory & Practice in Rural Education*, *9*(2), 20–34. https://tpre.ecu.edu/index.php/tpre/article/view/21

Wood, R. J. (2020, December). The stubborn classicism of classical music: What critics get wrong about the genre's longstanding diversity problems. *The New Republic*. https://newrepublic.com/article/160469/insidious-classism-classical-music

Yosso, T. J. (2005). Whose culture has capital? A critical race theory discussion of community cultural wealth. *Race Ethnicity and Education*, *8*(1), 69–91. https://doi.org/10.1080/1361332052000341006

Yow, W. Q., Sou, K. L., & Wong, A. C. (2024). A novel dual-language touchscreen intervention to slow down cognitive decline in older adults: A randomized controlled trial. *Innovation in Aging*, *8*(7), Article igae052. https://doi.org/10.1093/geroni/igae052

For Product Safety Concerns and Information please contact our EU
representative GPSR@taylorandfrancis.com
Taylor & Francis Verlag GmbH, Kaufingerstraße 24, 80331 München, Germany

www.ingramcontent.com/pod-product-compliance
Lightning Source LLC
LaVergne TN
LVHW012336130926
847902LV00028B/411
* 9 7 8 1 0 3 2 7 9 8 0 6 6 *